W9-BTK-719

Dr. Rimaletta Ray

Method of the Right Language Behavior

Language Intelligence

Or

Universal English

Remedy Your Speech Skills

Book 3 / Practical Part

Be Language–Fit to Succeed!

Copyright © 2013 by Dr. Rimaletta Ray.

ISBN: Softcover   978-1-4836-7443-8
                    Ebook   978-1-4836-7444-5

All rights reserved. No part of this book may be reproduced or transmitted in any form or by any means, electronic or mechanical, including photocopying, recording, or by any information storage and retrieval system, without permission in writing from the copyright owner.

This book was printed in the United States of America.

Rev. date: 08/19/2013

To order additional copies of this book, contact:
Xlibris LLC
1-888-795-4274
www.Xlibris.com
Orders@Xlibris.com
139862

Contents

Part 3 – Remedy Your Reading Skills *(Speech Odyssey)*   137

Mental Skills are just as Trainable as your Physical Ones"

(Discover, Jan. 2011)

English is Ruling the World!

You are Ruling Your English!

Book Three

Speech Odyssey / Speech Skills

Remedy
Your
Speech Skills

Speaking, Writing, Reading, and Listening Skills

Language Competence + Speech Performance!

English is Ruling the World!

You are Ruling Your English!

Part 1

Speech Odyssey / the Art of Speaking

The Art
Of
Speaking

Speaking Skills in Focus

**You are what you Say, and you Say
what you are!**

English is Ruling the World!

You are Ruling Your English!

Modes
Of
Speaking!

Information for Consideration

Information is Ammunition!

Chunk 1

The Art of Speaking Correctly!

Brain cells program the language; mind fields radiate thoughts, and vocal cords produce speech. The science needs yet to figure out how brain cells process information that we voice out later. In our increasingly electronics-based society, language skills are certainly number 1 aptitude. If your language is rich in vocabulary, if it is professionally-oriented, apt, correct and not too wordy, you are at advantage in any domain of life. We are actually living at the time of new **language monitoring techniques** that we also are trying to explore and develop here. Language habits that we have been remedying so far have a progressive, accumulative nature; speech skills have a result-oriented nature. Let's focus on them now.

Language acquisition is a process; speech performance is the result of the brain work. In other words, you need to develop grammar habits and speech skills in touch that is, practicing both **simultaneously.** The new time, technologically- advanced and very speedy, dictates a new way of thinking, feeling, being, and speaking. **We need to break the stereotypes** of **whatever saying and hullabaloo speaking** to build up new strategic thinking and very controlled, economical, one-pointed speaking. In other words, to utilize language information, we need to control our speech, targeting the state of flowing of language and speech, which we call fluency.

The problem is, **we need to teach our language brains to get rid of dissipated thinking** that always results in an inadequate self-expression in speaking. It ruins our brains and, therefore, life. Obviously, the quality of your English is the passport of your mind. Every language teacher is, in fact, **a language programmer** that programs the language in your brain so that your speech actions were not automatic when a particular language situation confronts you.

Remember, the erosion of the language leads to the disruption of speech. Your mind is constantly in a speaking mode. One thought goes after another, non-stop, without any prior planning, unless you start paying conscious attention to your thoughts and put them in control. As is mentioned above in *Part 2, Remedy 61,"Language Monitoring,"* **it is essential for you to establish a tight control over every sentence you**

say or write because your brain channels you from conscious control of the correctness of your speaking to the unconscious, uncontrolled " **free range" speaking**. However, this becomes possible only if you go through the first stage of language healing and follow the rules of the right behavior for quite a while. That is why we keep drawing your attention to the idea of changing bad mental patterns that generate wrong speaking and turning them into good ones that will facilitate controlled, **conscious framing of your thoughts.** Lan7guage control does it! So, **think before speaking!**

Space for Notes:

• Brain has the capability

wordy –
hullabaloo –

Focus on One-Pointed Speaking!

Chunk 2

Language - Speech Coherence

Throughout the book, we kept pointing out to you repeatedly the importance of developing the connectivity between your left and the right brains as the main goal of the remedial work on your English. Let us remind you again that **disconnectedness hurts your language personality** which in turn ruins your self-esteem, essential for developing your speaking skills without any hindrance.

The thing is, you are what you say, and you say what you are! "Logos" has two meanings in Greek. Logos is thought, and Logos is speech. Apparently, they are inseparable. **There is no speaking without thinking!** But thinking is a skill that has to be learnt, especially when thinking has to be developed in a foreign/ second language. At the outset of your second language learning, there is no path in the brain. We walk across the field of a new language and only a slight imprint is made. Then we walk the same way a few times more and, eventually, a trail begins to emerge as a shot-cut in your brain. **Momentum Builds!**

Gradually, the right trails of the language use in the brain are formed thanks to a thorough sorting out of the language information and its logical organization for a conscious perception of the material under study. These shot-cuts get wired in a learner's brain thanks to a thorough sorting out of the language information and organizing it into special digestible, highly logically connected modules of language information that we call **"Chunks"** here.

Once the mentality starts taking shape, it is critically important **to monitor the language information, stored in the brain through its special systematization and simplification** that allows for the information to be integrated consciously and to affect rightly your speech performance.

The right thinking = correct speaking! These goals can be accomplished thanks to your establishing **a tight control over the right language behavior,** and you are being reminded of that in each part of the book. Without such control, we stand to be at the mercy of technology because the use of **the language becomes totally casual, mechanical, and barely controlled on the Internet,** not to mention a very chaotic speaking in face-to face communication when the interlocutors often hardly care for the form of the language, trying to communicate the content of their thoughts uncontrollably.

Therefore, **disciplined language learning remains to be a necessity** because it develops the ability to reason properly in a second language. Like we are unable to solve any mathematical task without knowing the formulas that need to be applied for the solution of the task, the second language learning needs to be brain-oriented and so that each piece of the information presented for learning could be connected with the one studied prior to that, **shooting new connections, and generating new idea.**

Space for Notes:

- connectivity between your left and right brains
- 'you are what you say and you say what you are"
- there is no speaking without thinking.
- the right thinking = correct speaking.
  - it can be accomplished
- Establishing a tight control over the right language behavior
- the use of language becomes: casual - Mechanical - barely controlled on the internet
- Second language learning → Brain oriented.

New information + Prior knowledge = new ideas.

Well-Thought is Well-Said!

Chunk 3

Cut the Umbilical Cord of the Native Language

The problem # 1 that we have mentioned in *Part 2, "Remedy your Grammatical Habits"* is the **unformed English mentality,** when the native language continues to dictate to you the direction of your thought. In this situation, the more you study, the less they know and understand. The freedom from this perpetual slavery to the native mentality dictate is in conquering and transcending oneself to finally **cut the umbilical cord which connects you to the central computer - the native language computer.**

A great saying, **"You are as many time s a man as many languages you know"** is absolutely right in its implication. However, speaking those languages in a hullabaloo way will not make you a great man. It will be cute, but not acceptable in a serious language environment. That means that you need to learn to think in English, experience the effect of your second language personality shaping, but retain your native individuality.

Be yourself, and think for yourself, but beware! **English thinking is different!** It is a one-way street in its grammatical structure. Just thinking in your habitual, native language way and using the English words in whatever way to express yourself in English will not work. *In Book Two, Section 2,"Remedy Your English Mentality,"* we point out to you how crucial it is for you to become **much better language aware.** Awareness equips the brain with the ability to channel your mind from conscious, meaningful control over every thought that you generate in English to, eventually, spontaneous, uncontrolled, and correct speaking. **No other way. Period!**

Your evolution in the second language is based on your ability to achieve **conscious individuality in the language,** in our case in English. Learning a new language or using the one you are blessed with is not something external. It is the product of your mind and, therefore, something you can and should control. **But you need to lean to manage both languages in a different way!** Your speaking in your native language constitutes an uncontrolled interaction, while the using of English needs to be controlled every speaking or writing moment for you to be able to establish first a mind-to mind, then- a "mutually intelligible communication".

Native language = uncontrolled interaction ⎫   *mutually*
                                                      intelligible
                                                      communication

Second language = controlled interaction ⎭   *mind-to-mind*
                                                      communication

We mean that you need to redirect your thinking from the native language route to the English one to obtain a desirable fitness in English. *(See Part 2, Remedies 1 and 2)*

Space for Notes:

Language Competence + Speech Performance!

Chunk 4

Levels of Speaking Skills

So far, we have talked about speaking skills development and the ways of a better self-expression in speaking in general. Now let's check with the section *"Second Language Consciousness"*, *Book One, Goal 3* for your reference. There are **five levels of language mastery in speaking** for you to empower. They are: **Micro, Meta, Mezzo, Macro, and Super,** the same ones that you go through, remedying any language habit or speech skill, or actually, any skills.

1. **Random Speaking - Micro-Level -** *This is the level of speaking with no conscious control. That is the lowest level of speech mastery, when the brain is not controlled by the mind at all. As a matter of fact, it's not ready to be controlled by the mind because* **the mind is totally channeled by the native language.** *A speaker uses some words, phrases, or disconnected sentences in a foreign language. This is normally the stage a learner of a new language will most likely acquire when working with Rosetta stone or any other language teaching business that promises surprising overnight results. Through the entire book, we keep emphasizing the importance of connectivity in the brain that takes time.*

2. **Framed Speaking - Meta-Level -** *This is actually* **prepared speaking,** *backed up by a written paper to refer to. Students' presentations in class are often prepared in advance, and they feel more comfortable reading them, rather than speaking flexibly on the topic in question. Such way of speaking is very popular because it is normally somewhat outlined. There is a very characteristic saying about this type of speaking." The best off-the head speaking is the one that is well prepared". The speaking skills are* **much more accurate grammatically,** *but are not solid yet.*

3. **Channeled Speaking - Mezzo-Level -** *This is the level at which good speaking skills are displayed by a second language user. The stage fright is overcome; there is flexibility of self-expression and there is much less dependency on a written back-up text. Speaking may be well governed by* **the conceptual vocabulary blue print,** *presented on the index cards for reference.*

4. **Conscious Speaking - Macro-Level -** *This is the level of very good speaking skills The speaking is fluent, accurate, free of stage fright, but it is* **consciously controlled** *governed by the rules of the right language behavior.*

5. **Masterful Speaking - Super Level -** *Fluent, logical, coherent self-expression in the second language.* **SL mentality is established in the brain.** *Thinking skills are solid and the language proficiency is not consciously controlled. It is close to that of a native language.*

Space for Notes:

Re-think the Entire System of language acquisition!

Chunk 5

Develop your Language Intuition

Obviously, you are going or have gone though all those stages, trying to perfect your English. Having established mental control over your English, you've given your brain a powerful signal about which kind of language behavior to move forward to. **But to become a conscious learner, you have to become a watcher of your language from within!** To obtain conversational ease, you need to establish a precise mental and emotional control over your English.

It's necessary for you to take an observer position of your speech performance. **Reflect on your language consciously.** If you manage yourself mentally and emotionally, the language will become better managed in you. Everyone manifests himself through his / her "**cerebral script.**" *(John Baineso)*

Speaking as any other skill has to be managed properly in your mind first. Do not speak on impulse. Overcome the inertia of empty speaking. It is harmful for the brain. Speaking with nothing to say contaminates your English. The present day world is governed by "**mechanical intelligence.**" Mechanical intelligence drives the speaking of many people. Correct, meaningful speaking is possible only in the state of intense wakefulness and full control over your speech.

Also, **work on the precision of words.** Have a mental picture of the words that you are learning in your mind. Always write the new words that you feel you might need down. Language intuition is linked to your subconscious mind that has the mental picture of this or that word you need. It is connected directly to the vocabulary stock in your brain. That is why it is crucial to have your vocabulary meticulously organized as we suggest in the part of the book that remedies your vocabulary habits.

Please be easy on yourself. Affirm your right language behavior to yourself and others as if it is so. Be proud of yourself for it! Maintain this attitude and your language intuition will not fail you. **You will receive a back up immediately.**

Remember, over 90% of our mental life is subconscious. If we fail to make use of this marvelous power, we condemn ourselves to live within narrow limits. Our subconscious processes are always life-ward and constructive. The subconscious mind is the builder of your language habits (pronunciation, grammar, vocabulary), and it maintains their right function. Therefore, your right language behavior depends on your language intuition. Mis-information in the language results in mis-management of speech. So, your inward feeling for what is the correct way to use the language channels your correct thinking in it; correct thinking generates correct speaking and writing. **You stop feeling yourself in the language and start feeling the language in you!**

Space for Notes:

Frame your Thoughts Consciously!

Chunk 6

Visualize Your Speaking

Your speaking is designed in the mental studio of your mind. It is done by your subconscious mind. There is always a direct response from the infinite intelligence of your subconscious mind to your conscious thinking. **The art of learning English is a technique or a process, and the science behind it is the definite response of your creative mind to the mental picture of your thought.** Unless there is first an image in the mind, it cannot move, for there would be nothing for it to move toward. So, the easiest and the most obvious way to formulate an idea is to visualize it, **to see it in your mind's eye first,** as vividly as if it were alive.

This process of thinking forms impressions in your mind. These impressions become manifested in words, sentences, phrases, texts. You visualize the type of word, sentence, phrase, text that you want to say.

This imagery and thought processes become a plastic mold, **a matrix,** from which the building of the thought will emerge. It may be right or wrong, but it always begins as visualization. If, for instance, I say the word "a pen", you, most likely, see the word "pen" in your mind or the image of a pen. Your **mental language imagery** is projected as if it is drawn or written down. The language building progresses until it stands vividly finished, conforming to the mental patterns of your mind, the architect of your thinking. *(See the goal "The Ultimate Result Vision", Book One, Goal 6)*

That is why stick this great saying: "**The best off the head speaking is the one that is well-prepared.**" Take some seconds to think before you start speaking, be it a simple response to your interlocutor, a small / big presentation in front of the class, or an important report at a business meeting. Your message on a phone, your texting or any other creative work in English, has to be properly organized, visualized and then produced.

Plan your speaking in advance. Pick and sort out the word-combinations that might represent your ideas. Structure them logically into an outline of your entire verbal utterance or a text. Keep the mental picture of what you are going to say in your mind. Visualize the vocabulary units that you have singled out to frame your thoughts. If you need to have a speaking presentation, be sure to write the blue print vocabulary of your ideas on index cards. *(See Book 2, Part 3, Remedy 55)* Have them in hand. It is a great back up for your speaking. You will be surprised how great you will sound and how much more confident you will feel about the way you sound.

Most importantly, be mindful of the ultimate result vision, **the URV,** of your work on the speaking skills. Your knowledge is lifeless if you do not impregnate it with the URV vision Otherwise, **the arrow of your attention will be deflected from its mark.** Visualize yourself speaking with a conversational ease, focusing on each step in this part consciously.

Space for Notes:

The Inner Language Vision is the
Speech Detector!

Chunk 7

Tame Your Tongue!

You need to become sensitive to every mistake you make and abstain from the verbal and written violation of the language rules. **You need to demonstrate some verbal wisdo**m. Set aside some time for **"tongue fasting"** or **cognitive control training.** As a matter of fact, your thoughts can make or break your speaking. The brain is the motor of its engine, the tongue is the steering wheel, and the mind is the driver. Together, they take you to the place of your destination. **Learn the art of saying the right words at the right time.** Actualize your emotional control Start resisting the temptation to say things quickly, this very minute.

Also, **language remedying needs character**. Be constantly at war with your mistakes, the polluters of the mind. I guarantee that at the end of the verbal fast, you will become linguistically empowered as you transform your tongue into a manageable tool for the right language behavior because everything you say will be based upon the rules of the language.

Self-monitoring has to be instilled in the brain by your desire to speak English correctly, on the one side, and the necessity to respect the rules of the language and your conversation partner's ears, on the other. The pleasure of speaking a foreign language spontaneously is great, but it gets doubled when you are able to do it correctly.

Remember, **speaking is the way to externalize our personalities.** It is the passport of our mind. **The brain works, the mind talks!** When you tame your tongue, or in other words, control your language, you help your mind to find the key to maintain your mental and emotional equilibrium. In fact, control is the junction point between reason and emotion.

The Junction Point= Control

Reason   Emotion

Finally, of course, the issue of the language control is connected with a language individuality that is like a blueprint that outlines the innate tendencies that are in our personal outlay. But these tendencies, whatever bad, can be empowered with the determination to display the correct language behavior. **Remember, a conscious speaker operates with emotional calm**. Control the power of your conscious speaking with your mental focus on the right language behavior! So, if we are learning speaking without self-expression, without self-control, you are teaching yourself **Janusian thinking,** Janus being an ancient Roman God with two faces, looking in opposite directions. Such thinking results in unconscious, automatic speaking.

Space for Notes:

Put Thinking in Charge of your Emotions!

Chunk 8

Beware - Elliptical English!

Another piece of valuable information is connected with **the phenomenon of conversatio**nal **English.** The thing is, an English sentence does not start without a subject or a verb in it, unless we are dealing with **Elliptical English** (an abridged sentence), very common for a colloquial speech. Then we tend to drop the subject, and sometimes the helping verb that goes next after the subject. Check it out.

E.g. **Glad to see you. = I am** glad to see you. / **Been there, done that. = I have been** there, **I have done** that. / What are you doing?"- **Driving. = I am driving.**

Hearing such elliptical sentences, an uneducated language-wise mind perceives it as a language norm, and, hence, we hear all sorts of incorrect English around. On the level of the content of the message communicated, it is quite understandable, but on the level of the form of the language, the person speaks and writes in absolutely broken English that is impossible to be fixed unless real clearing of the mess in the brain takes place on the conscious level.

Very often, it is hardly possible to be done on your own. You need guidance, and this is what we provide here. You need to learn the art of correct language flowing, or the art of the right language behavior. **Apparently, to be out- spoken does not mean to have a diarrhea of speech, or speaking in a hullabaloo way.**

People, speaking English like a foreign language, often pick up wrong language patterns, dictated by the native language environment. They get involved in **the vicious circle of wrong language behavioral standards** that get activated by the unconsciously, or automatically learning mind. To a certain extent, the wrong speaking environment that is channeling such uncontrolled speaking consequently represents itself in writing, too. It becomes what Carl Yung called "**collective unconscious.**" Even though Yung uses this term to qualify the state of the society's consciousness, we can well apply it to wrong, sporadic speaking heard everywhere.

As culture shapes a man, so language use shapes a man's mentality, often making it linguistically and therefore psychologically pathological. Such speaking develops an unconscious language personality, and **the pathological language speaking** hurts the ears and mind of those that respect their language, intelligence, and culture. Only language awareness gives you the second wind in speaking because only conscious perception of knowledge can demonstrate what is right or wrong

1. *You welcome. - You are welcome.*

2. *Gotta do it. - I have got to do it.*

3. *Hope so. - I hope so.*

4. *Where you going? - Where are you going?*

5. *Wanna go there? - Do you want to go there?*

6. *Sounds like fun.- It sounds like fun.*

Space for Notes:

Knowledge makes it Perfect!

Chunk 9

Brain Talk

Next, let's summarize the main concepts that we promote here to help you master **the right language behavior in English.** To obtain conversational ease in a foreign language, we need to set up an entirely different set of neural signals in the brain. We made it clear above that the whole art of speaking correctly is in **overcoming a bad habit of uncontrolled speaking**. Mechanical speaking is produced by infinite combinations of mechanics of thought in a hypnotic state of speaking spontaneously, on momentum, often acting with a kind of speed, born out of desperation.

Actually, when you are in a foreign country where English is the only source of communication for you, such behavior might work. However, if you choose to live in the language or to use it as a vehicle for professional success, **self-regulated speaking is a must.** You absolutely need to zero in on the minor peculiarities of the language to get accurate speech

The goal is to reunify your tongue and the mind! The thing is, uncontrolled speaking or writing develop pathological trails in the brain and cause **mental language malfunction**. So, the process of rationalizing speaking is the name of the technique of the Method of the Right Language Behavior. **Do not allow yourself erratic language behavior that results in messy speaking**. Pay conscious attention to the logical connection between your thoughts, the framing of those thoughts in the correct tense form, the use of the articles, prepositions, intonation, the stress of the words, and their correct pronunciation.

There are no trifles that can go uncontrolled. **One mistake in the electrical circuit of the brain results in the breach in the whole light system of thought.** The problem is that chaotic grammar appears later to be so difficult to fix that a student stops to care or does not care to delve beyond the surface of the language. Hence, the language intellect gets driven in the attic as insignificant and useless. A student hopes to reach clarity without any effort, by magic. Since often English learners hate effort; easy magic has an extraordinary attraction.

Taking higher levels of college English doesn't work, either, because a student builds up further knowledge on the prior chaos. **Order can and**

should be manifested in the brain for the correct language behavior, be it in a native language or a foreign one. What's interesting is that order requires a mediator or an intermediary. Chaos was obtained by a learner without a mediator. An instructor or a learner's aware attention consciously applied each time he wants to say something can act as a mediator, but **the remedial work has to be dome zealously from scratch.** This work requires a new self-image, an objective vision of the identified language in oneself. In contrast to a subjective vision of the unidentified language in oneself! Here's where we come to help.

Space for Notes:

Do the Language Remedial Work from Scratch!

English is Ruling the World!

You are Ruling Your English!

Section 2

Speech Odyssey / Speaking Techniques

The Choreography

Of

Speaking

Speaking Techniques

The Brain Works, the Mind Talks!

Remedy 1

Speaking vs. Writing

Speaking and writing, being two different types of communication, demand two different approaches to the development of their operative skills. Both types of communication demand creating the language from inside out, that is with full attention to the language correctness and grammatical precision. So, the comments like: "It's OK to make mistakes. Just keep talking. Practice your English; Don't pay attention to your mistakes." are very harmful for the progress of language transformation because **bad language patterns become chronic. They inhibit your intelligence and lower your potential.** Bad language habits generate "a stage fright", the fear of speaking in public that is very destructive in its essence. Stage fright is the result of unhealed residue of language damage done to you. Check out our tips please.

Speaking

1. **Speaking is a free lance thinking! It creates an emotional personality.**

2. **Speaking is a spontaneous act of making meaning**. The content of the message is mainly controlled by the brain.

3. **The technique of question- answer work** needs to be managed. (*See, Part 4, Remedy the Speaking Skills, Types of Questions*) **The indirect word-order** in a question is a must!

$$V1 + s + V2 + O = P + T? \text{ / Would you like a cup of coffee?}$$

4. **Responsive skills** have to be absolutely managed. English is a responsive language. You need to verbalize your response to what your conversation partner says. Just a nod of the head is not enough. E.g. Do you believe it is possible to be done? - **Pretty much.**

Writing

1. **Writing is a disciplined thinking. It creates a thinking personality.**

2. **Writing is a synthesizing act of making meaning.** You need to control both the form and the content of the message that you communicate with your writing.

3. The **direct word-order** has to be observed by all means. **(S+ V+ O+ P + T)**

4. **The Sequence of Tenses in narration** has to be controlled. (*See Part 3, Remedy the Writing Skills*)

Space for Notes:

Grammar is the Modus Operandi
of communication!

Remedy 2

Brain Works, Mind Talks

Next, go back please to *Chunk 4* that presents the levels of your language awareness. Alongside with the tense system, you need to remedy your sentence structure in English at this physical dimension of language awareness.

We are sure that very often, when you speak or write in English, you tend to mix up sentences, messing up the ideas and making your English incorrect. It always happens when your emotions overflow your reason, and you stop controlling your English for its correctness. That's a very common mistake. That's, actually, one of the reasons why we write about **the importance of emotional intelligence in the second language learning**. But you will be able to address this language issue a little later.

Naturally, **messy speaking gets reflected in messy writing**, and vice-versa. It happens because your brain is constantly working in a speaking mode. You never stop talking to yourself. Such talking is called **inner communication.** You need to be in charge of your thoughts, or to be in control of your **outer communication** with the world, or verbal communication.

Verbal communication or speaking is usually more flexible and less mind-controlled because it is content-governed, not the form of the language. You want to control it, anyway! Your American friends, most likely, do not correct you when you speak casually and make mistakes in your grammar because they perceive your English **on the level of its content** of what you are saying, or, in other words, the meaning of what you are saying.

The form of your speaking, that is the structure of your speech, or its grammar, is of less importance in verbal communication. **The content of your speech is at play!** So, people get you at the level of the content, and they often do not care for your grammatical errors. You may even earn a compliment, "Your English is cute."

Written communication, however, should be very controlled! Writing is speaking to the mind, and the mind needs to follow the language structure and grammar because the comprehension of your piece of writing by a reader depends fully on the way you structure your thoughts and the way you arrange them grammatically. **The form of the language is at play in written communication.**

So, be constantly aware of the sentence structure in your English. The right sentence structure helps to channel the English language in your brain correctly. This is what forming an English mentality in your brain means.

Space for Notes:

Be Language Aware and Speech Competent!

Remedy 3

Grammatical Differences at Work

Speaking and writing are the two major types of Communication which is the process of encoding, the act of sending messages and decoding them. In order to systematize your language effectively, we need to consider not only the differences between acquiring the native language and a foreign one, but also the types of communication, **Speaking and Writing,** in which we are using the language. The whole art of speaking and writing correctly is in overcoming bad language / speech habits that corrode the language. **Muddled thinking is the diagnosis for such language disease.**

The two types of communication have **different grammatical, lexical, and organizational characteristics** that greatly affect your speaking or writing in English correctly. We will talk about each of them in opposition in **Part Two** of the book that will address the ways of remedying the basic speech skills- **Listening, Speaking, Reading, and Writing.** Meanwhile, let's focus on some of the differences that the RLB method brings to your attention in this book. Let's focus on some of them. The techniques of Speaking and Writing are different!

Speaking

1. **Speaking is a very flexible type of communication that is governed by the content of the message that** is being communicated, not so much by its form. *For example, when you communicate with an American in English, you often mess up the tenses, miss the articles, use wrong prepositions, etc, However, the total comprehension of what you are saying is still being perceived, and it is done on the on the content level. Your interlocutor is not bothered by the fact that your grammar is incorrect. He/ she understand what you are communicating to him in general, and he does not think it to be appropriate to correct you, unless you ask for being corrected.*

2. We also use a lot of **Elliptical English or** *shortened forms of speaking, when the helping verb, the subject, or even almost the whole sentence are dropped in a casual conversation. It is called conversational or elliptical English.*

Eg.- How you doing?- Great, thanks.

- My battery's out. - **Been** there, **done** that. (I have been there, I have done that.)

3. We also use a lot of contracted forms of the helping verbs

Eg. - **I'll** call you. - **I'd** rather do it tomorrow.

4. **Speaking is a very emotional type of communication.** *It creates an emotional personality, so managing your emotions is so crucial. in verbal communication. We also use different interjections to express our emotions, as well as different types of intonation.*

Eg - **Wow!** (to express admiration);- **Ouch!** (to point to pain) etc.

(For more information on the emotional English check the book "Americanize Your Language, Emotionalize Your Speech, www. novapressnet)

5. We may **speak non-stop**, or do as the Americans say "Blah, blah, blah …", *but the essential part of communication- the interaction- will remain functioning and we will communicate our message, anyway. If need be, we can ask a person to repeat his statement for us to comprehend him / her better.*

6. Most importantly, **speaking is a two ways, non-mediated communication. It is a Subject-to-Subject** communication, **a dialog.** It's more tactical in its framework because it is spontaneous and less disciplined. You go with the flow of your partner's mind.

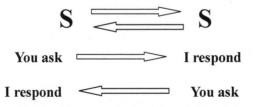

7. **Speaking is also the passport of your personality.** *It says a lot about your character, your knowledge, your education. Speaking develops your **auto-personal and interpersonal skills**. It is governed by the content of the message that you want to communicate, therefore, there is often little*

concern, if at all, is given to the form of the language by many second language speakers.

Writing

1. As apposed to speaking, **writing is a very rigid type of communication.** *Writing is governed by* **the form of the language, the blueprint** *upon which the content that is needed is communicated. The accuracy of your language is crucial in writing.*

2. **Writing is more strategic in its frame-work, too.** *It is governed by* **the master concept** *that you need to communicate to your reader; it develops your strategic personality, organizing your mind and communicating your message in a very specially-structured form.*

3. **Perception of your message, or the content of your writing depends very much on the form of your writing,** *and it is more important than your intention to say something to somebody. The rule that applies to writing is,* **"Perception is more important than intent!"** *The perception of your message by a reader develops very much on the how you present it both* in *form and in content. Therefore, writing is a holistic form of communication (See Section Writing Skills in Book Four "Speech Focus").*

4. **Writing is a one-way communication, a monolog, a subject - object - subject** *communication, mediated by an object of communication, the text. The written text (an essay, a story, a novel, a note, etc.) is* **the intermediary** *in the written communication. That is why writing is a mediated type of communication.*

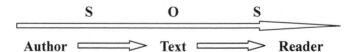

5. **Writing is also a very orderly and disciplined type of communication.** *You need to observe the order of words, the types of sentences that you are building, and the richness of the vocabulary you are using. It's the disciplined factor of writing in English that made English the language of the computers. Interestingly, English is the language that can be mathematically presented.* **It is a one-way street language**

$$a + b = c \quad \text{or} \quad S + V + O + Place + Time.$$

I have a cup of coffee at home every day.

Many other languages have a flexible word-order. You can start a sentence in a very care free way. It is not possible in English! Isn't it an amazing language? There are many more features that make English the language of the computers, but we will take a look at them gradually, while working on your Language Habits (Pronunciation, Grammar, Vocabulary) and your Speech Skills (Listening, Speaking. Reading and Writing).

Now that you know a little more about how you learn the language and use it in communication, you need to understand and to visualize the steps that you need to take to accomplish the goals of remedying your English and building up a solid English mentality

The goals of the right language behavior are presented in their hierarchy *in Part Three* of the book that follows next. So, come up with as many sentences in the 5 main tenses as you can, but be sure that you do not just make up examples with those tense. That is a regular practice in any grammar text book. **Be sure you do it with aware attention.** There is no Correct Writing without Correct Speaking!

Rationalize your Speaking to get better Writing!

Remedy 4

Dialogue vs. Monologue

Speaking is an interactive, **two-way communication.** It is a question-answer work that requires a certain technique. Actually, we deal here with two different ways of communication in speaking: a dialogue and a monologue. We are constantly in a dialog with some one or with our own thoughts.

A dialogue is **a subject- to- subject, bidirectional, unmediated communication**

You might want to look through Remedies 1 and 2 again in which we present the main differences between speaking and writing in terms of their grammar. The thing is, a dialogue has the characteristics of speaking, and **a monologue,** which is **a prolonged speaking**, has the peculiarities of writing, but is the form of speaking, anyway.

You need to observe the techniques of a question-answer work in a dialog. Your response depends totally on **your conscious self-monitoring** of the question. You need **to hear the helping verb** in it first because the helping verb carries the grammatical meaning of the main verb that you translate.

E.g. **Did** you get your car from the car dealer's yesterday- Yes, I **did.** / **Have** you paid your bills this month? - Yes, **I have.** / What **do** you do in the evening? - **I read or watch TV.**

A monologue in speaking is a subject-to-subject, one directional communication. You use this type of communication when we report on the events that we witnessed, when you make a presentation in class on any topic a professor assigns to you., or when he or she is lecturing in class. You speak in a monologue way when you talk casually to a friend on the Internet or when you text some one in a prolonged way, **without immediate feed-back.**

$$S \Longrightarrow S$$

You absolutely need to hear the tense form of the main verb in the question, or **its grammatical meaning** to be able to respond correctly that is in the same tense! Unfortunately, in an emotional situation, we often forget to pay attention to the helping verb and answer in a whatever way because the general content of communication is based on the meaning of the main verb that we easily understand, often disregarding the grammatical form it was used in. **That's a huge mistake in speaking,** and you don't want to keep making it. So, pay aware attention to the helping verbs in speaking; they carry the grammatical meaning. Be in control!

Here is an example of a small dialogue

-Hi, how have you been?

- So far, so good. Thanks for asking. By the way, what's new with you?

- I got promoted and I bought a house.-

- Good for you! You deserve it!

Below is an example of a small **monologue.**

Listen to what happened to me today. I was pulled over by a policeman who gave me a huge ticket for making a wide turn. I don't actually remember having made that big of a turn, but the policeman wouldn't listen to me. I told him that I was very much in a hurry to a doctor's appointment, but that didn't work, either. Then I tried to talk him into forgiving me for that turn just once, and I promised I would be more attentive next time, but he handed me a huge ticket through the window and drove off.

In writing, a monologue is a different type of communication. **It is subject-object-subject, one directional communication, mediated by a written text.** As a matter of fact, every book is actually a writer's monologue with his readers in which he communicates his message to them.

$$S \Longrightarrow O \Longrightarrow S$$

We will be remedying the written type of communication in Part 3 of the book. Meanwhile, note please that your writing skills in English are an absolute reflection of your speaking skills. Therefore, we are trying to draw your attention to fundamental differences between them. Both types of communication are regulated by the language awareness that you have worked on in *Book Two*.

When you are **speaking in a monolog way** at the presentation, say, making a report at a business meeting, telling a story to a friend, you are engaged, as a matter of fact, in **a verbal writing.** Such speaking requires a lot of **thought awareness management. You need to channel your thoughts according to the master message of your speaking discourse.**

In contrast to writing, your speaking may be interrupted with a question, or you might want to make an explanation. In any case, the grammar of your speaking will have to follow **the direct word- order** of writing, follow the sequence of tenses, and indirect questions peculiarities. *(See Part 2, "Speaking vs. Writing and the "Trouble shooting sections.)*

Space for Notes:

Self-Regulate Your Speaking!

Remedy 5

Four Types of Questions in English

Now that you have accumulated much knowledge about how language works in the brain, we need to try and put in order the simplest structures in it. So, do not grudge the time to go over the micro-level of the language with its simplest **Question-Answer work.**

There are four types of questions in English. Let's go over them for you to be able to operate them correctly. In the **Trouble Shooting** section" **Impeccable English**, you will be able to focus your attention on the 5 main tenses in English and different life situations that manifest themselves in a question-answer way. They are very helpful for your right language behavior.

1) "Yes / No" Question

a) **"Yes / No" Question** *The word-order in the "Yes/ No "question with the verb to be as the main verb is:*

$$V + S + O + P + T \ ? = Verb + subject + object + place + time?$$

The answer to such a question has to be short. The verb "to be" has to be in the same tense form, the intonation should be **the Rising Tone.**

E.g. **Are** you at home on Sundays? - Yes, I **am** (The Simple Present tense)

Were you at work yesterday? - Yes, I **was.** (The Simple Past tense)

b) **"Yes / No" Question** *with other verbs and in different tenses:*

$$V1 + S + V2 + O + P + T \ ? = A \ helping \ verb + subject + a \ main \ verb + object + place + time?$$

Will you be around tomorrow? - Yes, I **will.**

Are you studying in the library now? - Yes, **I am.**

Have you bought any food for lunch? - No, I **haven't.**

Did she see the doctor yesterday? - Yes, she **did**.

2) Wh. Question

This question is also called **the information question**. It starts with the question words and it requires a full answer. Remember, **you need to pay conscious attention to the helping verb** in **the Wh. Questions**, when you hear them. Without your noting the helping verb that carries the grammatical meaning of the main verb; you cannot answer the question correctly. The 5 most frequently used Wh. Questions are: **Who? / What? / Where? / When? / Why?**

The word order in the **Wh. Question** with the verb **to be** as the main verb is:

$$\textbf{Wh} \text{ word} + V + S + O + P + T ?$$

Please check out the Section" *Impeccable English", Trouble Shooting, Remedy 1, ID Information.* e.g. What country are you from? - I am from Denmark. The word- order in the Wh. Question with other verbs is:

$$\textbf{Wh.} \text{ word} + V1 + S + V2 + O + P + T ?$$

It's easy to start remedying your Wh. Questions, following the word-order in a sentence.

1. - The question to a subject-E.g. Who lives in Stamford?- I do. / Who **is** ready for this job?- I am. *The word-order is direct in the question to the subject and the verb has to be in the form of the #d person singular. The answer is short. E.g.* **Who** wants coffee? - I do. / *Who* is calling, please?- Mr. Brown is. The subject has to be accentuated in the answer.

2. - The question to a verb E.g. - **What** are you doing? -I am driving home.

3. - The question to an object in a sentence here - What have you bought? I've bought a pen.

4. - The question to the modifier of place - Where did you see him last?- I saw him at work.

5. The question to the modifier of time - When did you see him?.- I I saw him yesterday.

It's vey important to remember **the intonation aspect** in a Wh. question. First, the most important word lexically is accentuated more than the rest of words in the question. The question also ends with **the Falling Tone.**

3) OR- Question

The third type of question is also called **the Alternative Question** or the **OR Question.** In such a question, the intonation first goes up (the rising tone is necessary in the middle of the sentence), then the voce drops down in the end of the sentence.

E.g. Are you a ↗ **nurse**, or a ↓ **doctor**? - I am a ↓ nurse.

Has he ↗ **bought** or ↓ **sold** his car? - He has ↓ sold it.

You can actually ask an Alternative Question to any part of the sentence that might be the center of your attention. E.g. Did John or Mary call me?.- Mary did.

4) Tag- Question-

This is the most conversational question. It may also be called the **Communication Question.** It's the easiest question to ask, too. There are three ways in which this type of question may be asked: Mind the negative helping verb in a positive sentence. It's always a good way to initiate a conversation with the Tag question. That's why it's the most commonly used question. Here's how you make a tag question. **Record yourself asking all kinds of questions.**

a) **Grammatically,** with the helping verb as a tag at the end of a sentence.

E.g. You like this music, **don't you?** / She didn't show up at work, **did she?**

b) **Lexically,** with the help of the word **"right"**

You like this music, **right?** - Yes, I do.

c) **With the help of the intonation.** This question is extremely usable.

E.g. You like this music? - Yes, I do. / You follow me? - Yes, I do. / Wanna do it?-Sure.

Let's be Wise and Improvise

Let's improvise with the four types of questions, asking them to the sentence written below. Check it out:

I check my emails at home every evening.

1. Yes / No question - Do you check your emails at home every evening?- Yes, I do.

2. Wh. Question - What do you check at home every evening? - I check my emails.

3. Or-Question - Do you check your emails at home or at work every evening? - I do it at home.

4. Tag Question- a) You check your emails at home every evening, don't you? - Yes, I do.

b) You check your emails at home every evening, right? - Right.

c) You check your emails every evening?- Yes, I do.

Next, try to improvise the 4 types of questions to the following sentences:

1. He is driving to Boston right now.

2. Nancy told us an interesting story.

When asking a question, Discipline your Mind!

Remedy 6

Question Words, Starting with "How"

Below are some question words that are very commonly used in the Wh. Questions. See how they work. Mind the word- order in the second question. It is equal in meaning to the question, starting with Why? = How come? Such questions are very colloquial in American English. In the section *"Impeccable English"*, Tips on the Questions at Hand, there are different situations for you to remedy your speaking skills. **Record yourself asking those questions**.

---

1. **How**?	*How are you doing?*
2. **How come?**	*How come you never called? (The word-order in this question is direct.)*
3. **How old?**	*How old is the child?*
4. **How far?**	*How far is the ocean from here?*
5. **How late?**	*How late could it be?*
6. **How hard?**	*How hard is it to operate a smart phone?*
7. **How fast?**	*How fast can you drive in the USA?*
8. **How long?**	*How long have you stayed in Europe?*
9. **How cold?**	*How cold is it in Russia in the winter time?*
10. **How often?**	*How often do you work out?*
11. **How many?**	*How many friends do you have?*
12. **How much?**	*How much money have you paid for it?*

---

13. **How badly?** | *How badly do you want it really?*

14. **How about?** | *How about taking a class in Spanish?*

15. **Whose?** | *Whose car is that?*

16. **What kind of...?** | *What kind of job is that?*

Space for Notes:

Question- Answer ease is Language in Control!

Remedy 7

Questions to all Parts of a Sentence

As you see, the technique of question-answer work is basic in communication. However, the ability to ask 4 types of questions in every tense and with any other grammatically charged structure is not enough. *This skill is addressed in the **Impeccable English** section.* You might want to check it, if you want to make your conversational skills less rusty. This remedy is going to focus on asking question to any part of the sentence, as we do it in life, when you are practically interested in everything around us. In this case, a good training practice is **to commit to the order of asking questions** first, that is commit to the word- order in an English sentence. **(S+ V+ O+ P + T).** Of course, we ask such questions randomly in life.

Below, **ask question to the subject in a sentence, to the verb. to the object, to the modifier of place, and to the modifier of time.** We will start with the YES? NO question and finish with a Tag question. Take a look at the sentence that we are going to explore. Pay attention how the words are accentuated in the answer. **Record yourself asking all kinds of questions.**

My brother plays video games at home every day.

1. **Yes/ No Q.**	***Does*** *your brother play video games every day?- Yes, he* ⇂ *does.*
2. Q. to the Subject	***Who plays*** *video games every day?- My* ⇂ *brother **does**.*
3. *Q. to the verb*	**What does** your brother **do?** - He plays video ⇂ games.
4. **Q. to the object**	***What kind of*** *games does he play?-He plays* ⇂ *video games.*
5. **Q. to place**	***Where*** *does your brother play video games?- He does that at* ⇂ *home.*

6. **Q. to the time**   *How often does he play video games?- He does that every ⇓ day.*

7. **Tag question**   a) *Your brother plays video games every day,* **doesn't he?- Yes, he does.**

b) *Your brother plays video games every day,* ⤴ **right?- Yes, he does.**

c) *Your brother plays video games every* ⤴ *day?-* **Yes, he does.**

Check *"Impeccable English", Trouble shooting section* for the questions to the adjectives, adverbs and other possible parts of a sentence. There are different life situations, presented for your question scrutiny in that section, too.

Space for Notes:

Improve Your Language Behavior!

Remedy 8

Indirect Questions

Alongside with the technique of the direct questions that we have just reviewed, there is another very common mistake that pollutes the speech of English speakers. This mistake is connected with asking an **indirect question**, that is a question with some introductory phrase these questions make our speech more explanatory. Here's **the math formula** for them;

Yes/ No question-$V_1 + S + V_2 + O + P + T?$ = Direct question

E.g. Is she taking a class in American English? = **Direct** question (Indirect word- order)

I don't know if + $S+V_1+V_2+O+P+T.$ = Indirect question **(Direct word-order)**

E.g. I don't know **if** she is taking a class in American English. (Direct word- order)

As you see from the examples above, a direct question has an indirect word- order and a question mark at the end of the question. In contrast, **an indirect question has a direct word order** in a sentence and **there is no question mark** at the end of it. Mind you, instead of the conjunction **if**, we may use all kind of question words if you interpret a Wh. question. E.g. I don't know **who** is taking a class in American English./. I don't know **what** class she is taking. / I don't know **where** she is taking this class. Etc. **Record yourself, saying the indirect questions below.**

Merge your Language Consciousness with Speech Spontaneity!

The introductory phrases for the indirect questions may be as follows:

1. **I'd like to know…**

2. **I have no idea…**

3. **Could you tell me…**

4. **I wonder…**

5. **Do you know who (what, where, when, why)…**

6. **God know who (what, where, when, why)…**

7. **Tell me who (what, where, when, why)…**

8. **Can you explain to me why…**

+ indirect question.

Space for Notes:

Do not speak on Impulse!

Remedy 9

Channeled Speaking

Life is based on the emphasis on immediate sense. The inability to produce it at the right place and at the right time immobilizes the brain, damages the psyche of a speaker, and hinders his self-expression. This is one of the reasons why students prefer speaking at their presentations with the notes at hand, which they are actually reading, rather than speaking freely with a charming ease of a language master. We try to beat this feeling of being un-rooted with the help of **the channeled speaking technique** that will help you feel safe and welcomed. *(See Types of Speaking, Remedy 13 below.)*

We encourage you to bone up on **conceptual vocabulary-oriented speaking** that provides the tapestry for your thinking and models your speaking. Remember the rule: **"The right thinking governs the right speaking!** "**Conceptually organized vocabulary** *(See the section" Remedy the Vocabulary Habits"above)* channels your thoughts in the right direction. Let's see how it works. To begin with, we need a topic to speak on. Let's take the mind-set that carries the idea of social courtesy. **Record the elaborating on it by channeling your speaking on the word-combinations below. Make up a sentence with each word-combination. Pursue the logic of your thought.**

To Be Interesting, one Needs to Get Interested!

These re the word-combinations that might channel you in presenting this idea:

1. To display interest in sb.

2. To address a person by his / her name

3. To show genuine interest in…

4. To give a person your full attention

5. To ask a [person's name again if you happen to forget it

6. To be polite and respectful

7. To be tolerant to a person's opinion

8. To smile and receive a smile back

9. To listen to be listened to

It's pretty easy to go by these word-combinations that are channeling your speaking:

To get a person interested in you, you might want to display your interest in that person first. Try to address the person by his / her name. Show genuine interest in the person's business (personal problems, life). Give him / her full attention. If you happen to forget his / her name, don't hesitate to ask for it again. Be most polite and respectful. If you happen to discuss something arguable, you should be tolerant to the person's opinion Try to smile and you will be sure to get a smile back. Most importantly, listen to be listened to.

Vocabulary Channels your Speaking!

Remedy 10

Let's Be Wise and Improvise!

Try to improvise another small monologue, talking about the things that you need to avoid in communication. Let's amplify the **topic of communication** on the negative side. **Record yourself.** Be self-critical while listening to your speaking. Conscious practice makes it perfect. Rerecord yourself again and again, if need be. Like the way you sound in English!

Things that make you a complete failure in communication

1. To avoid staying invisible in a conversation

2. To use people's nicknames

3. To be too familiar, disrespectful

4. To be to cavalier or negligent with someone

5. To interrupt somebody without excusing oneself

6. To cut somebody short with a negative statement

7. To be insincere, condescending or arrogant *8. To be personal and nosy*

Next, talk about **the necessity to get well organized for college studying**. It's much easier to channel your thoughts with the vocabulary back- up, connecting them logically, right?

College Time, do not Whine!

1. To be a college student

2. To be prepared academically

3. To do well in college

4. To have self-discipline

5. To learn a new routine

6. To take the responsibility on oneself

7. To think for oneself

8. To do the planning

9. To take the learning seriously

10. To be committed to success

11. To work hard

12. To make new friends

13. To have a social life

14. To enjoy college time

Overcome the Inertia of Empty Speaking!

Remedy 11

Briefing Somebody on the News

"Language is not just the way you communicate with the world; it's the way you interpret the world in your mind." Apparently, talking about the news is a great activity that expands your social network and the general outlook. English is now called "Globbish" not only because it is the language of the globe, but also because it unites us in our speaking about the global affairs on the Internet. **Start a conversation with making an interesting statement,** expressing your opinion on something or ask a tag question to engage your conversation partner in a conversation. Here are some ice-breakers and possible responses to keep the conversation going. **Record yourself, saying that.** Like the way you sound in English!

Ice- Breakers: $\Longrightarrow$ Responses:

---

1. I'd like to brief you on...

- *Yes. What's going on there?.*

2. Could you update me / us on...?

- *No problem. What are you interested in?*

3. I'd like to talk about the situation in...

- *Great. What about it?*

4. Have you watched the latest news about...?

- *Yeah. Isn't it horrible?*

5. Has anyone heard the news about...?

- *No, what's going on there?*

6. What do you make of the situation in...?

- *I think it's interesting (weird, confusing).*

7. Have you heard the latest news about the Hurricane in...?

- *Oh, it's heart- breaking!*
- *Yeah, it's outrageous, isn't it?*

---

8. I'd like to comment on...   *- Go ahead. We are all ears.*

9. You know what, guys,   *- That's a real issue, isn't it?*
   the CNN featured
   the latest developments in..   *- Sorry, could you fill us in?*

10. There is a word that ...   *- Yes, looks like they are intending
                                        to...*

Space for Notes:

Work on the Fluency of Self-Expression!

Remedy 12

Small Talk American English

The Universality of English calls for the quality of your **Responsive Skills!** Don't speak toxic, second hand English. Don't stigmatize yourself with the inability to respond correctly. Be aware that **American English is the language of verbal responses.** When speaking in another language, you might want to express your understanding just by nodding your head or having an eye contact with the other person.

When speaking in American English, however, you need to be verbally active and respond promptly and accurately. For example, by just saying "Right", you give your conversation partner support, even though it might seem to you to be out of place to say that, **The lack of the responsive skills in English is one of the main reasons for many learners of English to feel tongue-tied, confused or totally lost in communication.** We can often see how people, speaking in English, are hurting language-wise because of their inability to make meaningful connections and to maintain a perspective of their message in speaking. When you lose this perspective, you hear the question, **"What's the bottom line?**

You might have noticed that in emotional situations you would rather speak in your native language because emotions are in the way of your immediate self-expression. Emotions remove the control of the mind, and you start speaking sporadically, in a desperate haste to express yourself. As a result, you start speaking toxic, uncontrolled English again.

So, the skills to timely react to your speaker's comments, as is having the necessary responses stored in your inner pocket is critical in communication, be it digital or face-to-face. In neuroscience, this wonderful ability is called **"Emotional Intelligence"** *(Daniel Goldman).*

My book **"Americanize Your Language, Emotionalize Your Emotions"** is addressing the problems of developing your responsive and emotional skills in English. We strongly advise you get it to better manage your second language, first intellectually then emotionally, in different life social situations. Here are a few examples for you to get an idea what Small Talk is all about.

You Say $\Longleftrightarrow$ **I Respond**

- Why don't we get together some day?

- *Sounds great. Give me a buzz.*

- Well, you've got some experience in this area, right?

- *Not really. Sorry to say that.*

Space for Notes:

Frame your Conversation with Small Talk!

Remedy 13

Conversation Starters and Ice-Breakers

The rule of Psycholinguistics is **"Say what you mean and mean what you say."** It has become extremely timely to follow. It is pretty difficult, though, to teach oneself this skill even in the native language, but it is not altogether impossible.

You need to put language and speech in synch, that is to start using the language consciously. In this speech remedy, we also need to put an accent on training your social skills that are the target of the previous speech remedy. In order to feel comfortable in conversational English, you need to learn to socialize with people properly and respond appropriately to what they say. You need to start a conversation and to handle digital communication correctly.

The Internet is loaded with American English expressions. In fact, American English is the door to the digital world in terms of Internet interaction and the variety of the new terms dealing with electronics. **But the art of socializing has to be studied, too**. Start with smiling and getting attuned to your speaker emotionally. Obviously, you need some verbal connectors to synchronize your integration with the conversation partner. They will help you expand your social network considerably. (*See the book "Americanize your English...")*

Verbal Connectors and Conversation Starters

1. For starters, I ...	*11. Apparently,*
2. Listen, John,	*12. Obviously,*
3. You know what...	*13. Naturally,*
4. Guess what...	*14. To make a long story short,*
5. For the record,	*15. The point is,*

6. Speaking of…

7. For your information,

8. The thing is,

9. Here's the thing,

10. Just so you know,

16. The bottom line is…

17. Why don't we…

18. Hear me out, please.

19. Bear with me, please,

20. Come on! Etc.

Space for Notes:

Recharge your Social Batteries in English!

Remedy 14

Keeping the Conversation Going

To keep the conversation going, you need to also focus on shaping your **Responsive Skills,** that is your ability to use **the language of verbal reaction correctly** When speaking in another language, you might want to express your understanding by nodding your head or having an eye contact with your interlocutor. Speaking in English, however, you need to be verbally active not to let the conversation die out. You need, actually, to learn to respond correctly and be alert for the conceptual venues of the conversation not to run out of it completely. Other than that, it's essential **to kick the ball of communication back to keep it going.** Here are some helpful tips

---

Conversation Back-Ups ⟹	**Possible Responses**
1. Speaking of…	*-Yes?*
2. I'd like to make a point here, if I may.	*- Sure.*
3. That's no issue, right?	*- I don't think so.*
4. I'd like to address the issue of…	*- Go ahead.*
5. Let's take a broader look at the situation.	*- Good idea.*
6. How does it sound to you?	*- Sounds great!*
7. It took me a while to get the hang of it.	*- I know what you mean.*

Wrapping the Small Talk Up

Finally, if you've run out of the conversation, just round it off, saying:

1. So much for it.	- *Thanks for your input.*
2. Thanks. it was great talking to you.	- *My pleasure.*
3. Let's call it a day for now.	- *Thanks, it was great talking to you.*
4. Let's finish our talk on a positive note.	- *I'm sure everything will work out.*
5. Let's come back to that problem later.	- *That's OK by me.*

Space for Notes:

Keep these Phrases in your Conversation Pocket.

Remedy 15

Small Talk Rules to Follow

To be a good conversationalist, follow the basic rules of any small talk. Record them for your speaking practice. **Recording is acting as auto-suggestion in this case**. Like yourself doing it.

To Be Interesting, Get Interested!

On the positive side, follow these rules: **(+)**

1. Show a genuine interest in somebody or something. Smile and receive a smile back.

2. Give people your full attention. Do not listen with pseudo attention.

3. Address a person by his last / first name.

4. Ask for a person's name again if you happened to forget it.

5. Be polite, respectful, and tolerant to another person's opinion.

6. Listen to be listened to! Be alert, focused, and connected to your conversation partner.

8. Display more tact and empathy during the conversation. Read the feelings of others.

9. Mean what you say, and say what you mean.

On the negative side, be sure to avoid: **(-)**

1. Staying invisible in a conversation.

2. Using people's nicknames and being too cavalier or negligent with some one.

3. Being personal or too nosy

4. Interrupting some one without excusing yourself

5. Putting somebody into a terrible spot in a conversation.

6. Do not speak in a robot-like trance: Blah, blah, blah...

7. Do not burden your partner with your Persona for too long!

Space for Notes:

Synchronize your Mind and your Tongue!

Remedy 16

The Art of Discussion

Discussion requires a conscious participation in a conversation and **establishing of a mind-to-mind contact with the speaker.** Also, taking control over your English is paramount. Then your brain will run like an efficient, quiet, cool-run natural machine. Stage fright is the most difficult obstacle to get rid of in a discussion. To keep the conversation going, you need **to manage your Small Talk responsive skills** that we have talked about above.

It's a good idea to master some conversation starters and **discussion back-ups** that we have for you below. The use of **the tag questions** to express supposition or to add up conceptually to a discussion is most helpful. You also need to have the responses of agreement and disagreement at hand. The book *"Americanize Your Language, Emotionalize Your Speech'"* provides an array of choices in this respect. Here are some of them for you to bone on. **Record these phrases in a meaningful context.**

1. I'd like to make a point about…. That's a real issue, isn't it?

2. I think it's critical (vital, crucial) that…, don't you think so?

3. What do you make of…? /. What's your take on…?/ What do you think about…?

4. There's no word about it, but I think that…/ Let me pick on the point that…

5. What do you think is a possible explanation to that? / What's on your mind…?

6. It makes sense, doesn't it? / It makes no sense, does it?

7. There is a lot of controversy about … / Turns out it is …

8. It strikes me as interesting to mention that… / I got to thinking that…

9. *I can't figure out why … / I'd like to bring up the point of…*

10. *How is that possible that… / What's your point on…?*

11. *Let's step back and see a bigger picture of the situation. / Let's round it off.*

Wrapping the Discussion up

. Let's round off our discussion with… /. Let's finish our talk on a positive (lighter) note.

. Let's call it a day for now. /. We'll come back to that problem later./ The bottom line is…

Space for Notes:

Be Immune to a Diarrhea of a Mouth!

Remedy 17

Speaking Venues

There are a lot of speaking venues to follow in any discussion. They are connected with the mental operations that we use in reading, writing, and speaking and that are mostly dealing with analyzing, synthesizing, and elaborating on the information that you operate with. To hit that target, you need to do some training of your **free speaking skills** along these lines, taking different **mind- sets as the food for thought**. There are many mind-sets for speaking or writing practices in the improvisational frame work on the pages of this book. Make use of them. Write them down into your note-book into the section "**Bank of Ideas."**

Life does not adjust to us, we adjust to Life!

Let's elaborate on…   *Let's expand on…*

Let's argue …   *Let's persuade that …*

Let's prove that…   *Let's infer…*

Let's picture…   *Let's wrap up our discussion of….*

Remember that vocabulary channels your speaking. So, before your start speaking along any of the **speaking venues** above, focus for some minutes on the topic vocabulary that might channel your thinking along the lines of the suggested mind-set. Record your speaking.

Let's Be Wise and Improvise!

1. To be tough   E.g. Life is, obviously, tough, but we should be tougher.

2. To overcome the obstacles in   We need to overcome a lot of obstacles in life.

3. To empower oneself with...	It's important for me to empower myself with self-esteem.
4. To adjust to life.	It's easier to adjust to life when you...
5. To live in the present	
6. To live in the present	
7. To focus on self-development	

Space for Notes:

"Put your Mind over the Brain!"

("Super Brain" by Rudy Tanzy)

Remedy 18

Design the Self-Talk in English

You know now that the most important thing for the right language behavior is to change the thought pattern. **Changing the thought patterns starts with changing your self-talk.** Self-talk is the endless stream of unspoken thoughts that run non-stop though your head every day. There is constant chatter and activity in your inner mind in the native language, but you need to **channel your self-talk in English.**

You thoughts can be positive or negative, logical or illogical, coherent, or incoherent. Some of your self-talk comes from logic and reason; others may arise from misconceptions that you had created due to your imperfect English before. That is why we have those **Psychological Corners** to back you up through out the book. They are meant **to boost your self-talk in the positive direction.** So, your steps on the way of conquering you self-talk to help your language transformation should go in accordance with the directions below:

1) **Your dominant thinking about yourself in English and English in you should be positive**. Keep saying to yourself. "I am doing great. I am thinking in English!'**Record your thoughts.**

2) Start practicing **intellectual stimulation in English.** By intellectual stimulation practices, we mean the habit of duplicating your thoughts in English or rather commenting on your actions inwardly to yourself in English every time you happen to remember about it. **The brain is very perceptive to persistence.** Keep doing it throughout a day. For example, you may think:

OK. I have finished my coffee. I am going to put together my stuff and head to the parking lot. Here I am at my car. Wait a minute. Where are the car keys? Oh, here they are. Now I am opening the car. I am starting the car engine. Great, it's working! I am driving now. I have stopped at the intersection. I am waiting for the lights to change. Let me go over the plan of action for the day meanwhile. First, I have to... etc. Here I go again.

This simple exercise will help you to live in the moment and to live in the language! It is extremely beneficial for the development of your thinking skills in English and your holistic language awareness. Willy-nilly, you need to think of both, **the form and the content of the language**, the grammar you are using and the vocabulary that frames your thoughts. This exercise if done religiously, will **change the tapestry of your brain** and will move your aware attention from the automatic reactions of hard drive of the reptilian brain to the soft ware of the frontal cortex, your thinking brain. It will also develop your **intuitive language skills in English** because this conscious exercise puts the mind of charge of your brain

Space for Notes:

Manage your Inner Voice in English!

Remedy 19

Control your English every Speaking Moment!

In Conclusion of this part, it is of paramount importance for you to be able **to see the whole domain of the language,** that is to take a systems view at every sentence you hear, read, or write. Language control means the ability to identify the correctness / incorrectness of your speaking in the entirety of the language system that, in a nutshell, we have presented in Part 3 of the book.

Establishing the wholeness and interconnectedness of the language habits and speech skills in the brain are the only prerequisite for a successful mastering of the language. Run your own brain consciously. Take the mistakes from its soft-ware and delete them. Don't sore them in your mental garbage bin. Only conscious mind is able to do it, and only conscious mind is responsible for an adequate verbal expression. Only conscious mind removes the self-inhibition and helps you establish the self-evaluation of the rightness or wrongness of the language actions you are about to implement. Thus, you will manage **to de-atomize your English** from the native language. Very soon, **you will have an inspiring sensation of your new feeling of the language thanks to you right language behavior.**

Note it please that repeated making of the same mistakes happens because you mind was conditioned for quite some time. Establishing a tight control over your thinking, speaking, and writing will teach you to respond to any language- speech bound situation **out of conscious presence.** Every consciously corrected mistake, or mindful, not automatic speaking / writing in English will be a true victory of the new mentality, of the **Second Language Consciousness** that will eventually become permanent with you.

Your thinking in English will be as natural as it is in the native language. That's the super level of language mastery, and you are going to get there. So, empower your English with discipline and control of the language rules that you are consciously aware of. In case of any doubt or absence of information on any subject, connected with your language habits or speech skills, feel free to get to our website" *Language Fitness.com.* We will fix any of your problems and help you stick further to the **Rules of the Right Language Behavior.**

Finally, say the inspirational boosters that we provide throughout the book and at the end of each part of the book. Doing so, you bring consciousness into your emotional mind and you practice emotional diplomacy *(See "Emotional Diplomacy" by Dr. Ray)* that will help you manage your emotions when speaking English.

Space for Notes:

Empower Bad Language Rituals!

Remedy 20

Don't Be Speech Bubbly!

Instructional Poem

Don't be speech- bub-

bly,

Recycle your poor vocabu-

lary!

Clean it of the words of profa-

nity,

Complaining, cursing, and va-

nity

Also, start rever--

sing

The words of hate into love in reher-

sing

For the true value of the words

Heard

Is often twisted into a verbal

Sword

That can kill, hurt, and in-

jure

More than any other weapon-like dan-

ger

"First was

    Word"

Is written on the Bible's

    Board!

                The word is also at the life's

                End

            When the words,"Finite a la Comedy!"

                Are said

True, life is "A Comedy of

    Errors"

That are reflected in the God's

    Mirrors

                But it would be much less,

                As such,

            If we were in charge of our words

                That much!

So, if you don't have something nice

    To say,

Keep the nasty words at your lips'

    Bay

            And put your unmanageable

                Tongue

            In the captivity of your mind's

                Run!

Remedy 21

Focus on the Outcome

We are done with remedying your speaking skills in terms of the main points that you need to consider to make your speaking in English more fluent and accurate. **The art of the right speaking is acquired only with practice and control** that are accompanied by aware attention to every word you say. We have noted above that correct speaking starts with conscious attention first and then gradually, after your speaking skills get rationalized, it becomes unconscious. It means that you do not have to control your grammar, vocabulary, pronunciation, intonation, etc. any more. Your speaking will be spontaneous and correct. Correctness will be rooted in the brain. But remember;

Only Conscious Practice makes it Perfect!

Having completed this part of the book, let's see what you've come to know about the directions in which you are going to perfect your speaking skills.

What did you come to know about...?

1. Language- speech coherence. What does it mean in your every day speaking practice? (Chunks 1,2)

2. The native language interference. How does it affect your speaking in English? (Chunk 3)

3. The second language intuition. How can you develop it? (Chunk 4)

4. What does visualization have to do with speaking? (Chunk 5)

5. What does the mind- set "Tame your Tongue!" imply in your native language and a second one? (Chunk 6)

6. Do you find speaking, boning up on the conceptual vocabulary blue print helpful? Feel free to get in touch with us through the website to show you how to single out the conceptually-loaded vocabulary from the text that you need to cover. Get in touch with us for any other purpose, involved with channeled speaking. (Chunk 7)

*7. What is **Small Talk**? Give an example of small talk in which you engage every day.*

*8. Comment on **the venues of** speaking that we need to deal with when mastering a foreign language speaking.*

Space for Notes:

Study the Art of Socializing!

Remedy 22

Psychological Corner

(Building up Personal Stamina)

Ending up the remedial work on speaking, we need to rekindle the entire system of language acquisition in order to maximize the effectiveness of language learning and boost your personal stamina that drives this learning and helps you manage your language better. Remember, if you cannot explain things simply, you don't actually understand them.

You may continue your remedial work on simple speaking skills in our trouble-shooting area, called *"Impeccable English'* at the end of the book. However, no matter what you do, you should remember that **at the center of the system of language learning is the self-image.**

Below, we give you a mind formula that will boost you success in language learning, and, actually, in everything in life. Keep saying to yourself though out the entire process of your working with this book the following mental program for success. **Boost your confidence and reinforce your every goal-setting with the following formulas**. Most importantly, believe in what you say to yourself.

"I am a strong, confident, and consistent master of my firm will.

I can…

I want to…

I will…!

I am becoming better and better in my Speaking Skills with each day!

Correct Speaking comes out of a State of Language Consciousness

The same mental program will back you up, both emotionally and psychologically, in your work at the pronunciation, in figuring out the grammatical structure of English or in the expansion of your vocabulary that is forming up your thinking in English.

You can apply it practically to anything. In this way, you will **re-educate your emotional brain that often hampers your self-expression in English.** To help yourself out emotionally, learn to be self-enthused. Just keep saying to yourself these words:

Space for Notes:

I can...; I want to ...; I will...!

Remedy 23

Language - Speech Profile # 4

With the completion of this part of the book, we want you to walk out of your past language speaking history with a sense of new accomplishment. It is fundamental to your understanding of your **self-concept in English.** You have a better idea of the road map that you will continue following to the quality English.

It is a controlled, action-filled, rational step in your English life. You are much more conscious of what you are rising to in the language.

You are learning to listen, speak, read, and write with a constant control over your English. So, take a minute and focus on the outcome of your work. **Do it in an auto- suggestive manner.** Record yourself.

Self-Assessment

*I have a better idea now of the main trouble spots in my pronunciation. I you have managed to reason out the English tenses. I am more conscious of my language errors while speaking, and I feel very good when I see them and correct them then and there. I do not let my language **slide to the automatic speaking or writing** with many uncorrected mistakes that pollute my English. I am doing great!*

Now, do the rating of your Language Habits and Speech Skills on the scale of **1 to 10**

Language Habits

1. Pronunciation Habits -

2. Grammatical Habits -

3. Vocabulary Habits -

Speech Skills

1. Listening Skills -

2. Speaking Skills -

3. Reading Skills -

4. Writing Skills -

Space for Notes:

I am Happy about Myself and the English in Me!

End of Part 2 / Speaking Skills

Part 2

Remedy

Your

Writing Skills

"Writing is the Algebra of Speaking"

English is Ruling the World!

You are Ruling Your English!

Section 1

Speech Odyssey

The Art
Of
Writing

Information for Consideration

Reflect on your Writing!

Chunk 1

You Write the Way you speak!

There is a wrong academic belief that learning English through primarily writing will make you a better speaker of English. It is absolutely true if we apply this approach to native language speakers. Writing, for sure, develops strategic thinking of a native born student, but it's the quality of speech grammar-wise that determines how you manage the language. The thing is, **the brain is constantly in the speaking mo**de. **What it says to you, you write.**

On the route of education in a native language, great **writing is the final step of the native language mastery.** Obviously, that is the reason writing of academic papers is so important for any educational purpose. Writing, no doubt, puts a learner on a new thinking critical track; it expands a student's outlook and shapes his/her thinking. There is no professional or personal growth without writing.

However, **a second language learner needs to learn to think and speak in English correctly first, before he/ she starts writing correctly.** The thing is, our brains are constantly in a speaking mode. We speak to ourselves non-stop. This **inner communication results in outer communication - the interaction with the world**. Naturally, if the inner communication in English is incorrect, messy, uncontrolled, the written communication will be a direct reflection of that mess.

Chaotic, unconscious, and uncontrolled language use can never build up a healthy language consciousness, no matter how many papers a student will be wiring in it. Other than that, continuous language learning at different levels, taking various language courses, or just self-studying can never result into the right language behavior unless this behavior is constantly conscious and permanently controlled for its correctness by the language carrier.

There should be no talking or writing **in a somnambulistic, casual, uncontrolled state of mind, triggered by emotions.** Emotion literally means "disturbance". A disturbed mind generates disturbed language. Bad language habits, generated by the bad language patterns in the brain disturb the intellectual self-expression of a language learner.

The suggested language and speech remedies that are recommended to you throughout our speech odyssey will back you up, both emotionally and psychologically.

We hope that having covered the remedial work on your grammatical habits and speech skills, you will feel better prepared to channel your thoughts correctly in writing.

Space for Notes:

Controlled Speaking Generates
Controlled Writing!

Chunk 2

Adjust the Train of your Thought!

Writing is a great intellectual stimulation, and the value of writing in shaping a second language learner's mind is immense. **Critical thinking skills** are the main skills that writing develops alongside with the organizational skills and therefore, strategic thinking. The greatest challenge lies in the value of thinking that your writing will reflect, and this is what you need to monitor.

Mistakes are big mental polluters in writing if there is no conscious language awareness to be guided by. An undisciplined, messy storage of vocabulary in the brain, as well as unconscious learning of grammar always result in **muddled thinking and messy writing.** As the proverb says, **"What is bred in bone will come out in flesh"**

First, pay attention to your incorrect English and immediately become aware of the mistake, made by you or anyone else. **Paying attention to the mistakes of others and inwardly correcting them** is another strep on the way of the conscious language learning. Eventually, you are developing the language feeling, or language intuition that will channel you along the language routes. Therefore, it's a good exercise to work on correcting the mistakes of others in speaking and writing. **Be language - insightful!**

Second, mind the English word-order and watch your English sentence structure. See to it that every sentence you say has a subject and a verb of their own. Say "No!" to irrational language conduct. **Switch on to aware attention**. Doing that, you change the cerebral script in your brain, governed by the mechanical thought action. **Get it channeled by the right language behavior, based on your language intuition**. This is what you need to develop with every speaking / writing action.

Third, do not connect each sentence with the conjunction "*and*", in a non-stop way *(and...and...and...)*. Speak in simple sentences to be on the safe side. Say or write one sentence at a time!. Do not connect more than two sentences into one compound or complex sentence. Remember, **"Less is more!"** So, manage the train of your thought in every sentence. **First think, and then write!** *(See Book Two," English Sentence Structure")*

Finally, establish a habit of self-observation in writing. With practice, the power of self-observation of the way you monitor the language in you will sharpen.

Also, if you feel a slightest trace of unwillingness or confusion about what to write, we ask you to take a break, to look through some materials that provide food for thought, sort out the vocabulary units from your"Vocabulary at Hand" notebook *(See the Vocabulary habits, Book Two)*, **organize your word-combinations conceptually** to channel your thoughts better, and then resume your writing.

Space for Notes:

No Compulsive Thinking / Speaking / Writing!

Chunk 3

Focus on the Form and the Content of the Language!

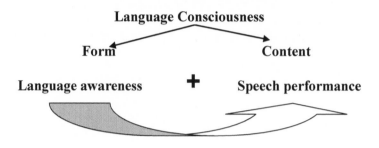

Conscious Connectedness

Any language learning has to be conscious and based on the unity of the language structure and its representation in speech. Unfortunately, due to the emotional turmoil caused by the necessity to say something quickly or to meet the due date in writing, most students alternate not between conscious and unconscious states of language use, but only between different levels of unconscious learning. Many students live in an almost continuous state of low level unease, discontent, boredom, and disconnection-a kind of background static.

So, it's essential for you to understand that the loss of conscious becoming in the language is the loss of being in it! You need to absolutely expand you English language consciousness, that is to constantly try and establish the connection between the form of your speaking/ wiring and the content of what you want to generate in your mind.

How? + What? = Form + Content

The quality of this unity is what shapes your language awareness and speech performance. By developing your language awareness and by establishing a tight control over your speech, both verbal and written, you are breaking bad mind patterns, **the old mode of language**

unconsciousness. It is a quantum leap in the evolution of your second language consciousness. Thus, you are learning the language with the present- moment awareness, and your mind becomes imbued with the sense of the quality of the language, or **the right language behavior.**

You will become aware of the eternal underneath of the form of the language, and therefore, will structure your speech (verbal/ written) easier, more accurately, consciously and fluently, with a deep sense of self-accomplishment. This is when **you will start seeing the language in yourself rather than seeing yourself in the language** *(See the Introduction to the book)*

Space for Notes:

Follow the Right Language Behavior!

Chunk 4

Levels of the Writing Skills

So far, we have been talking about writing as a great means for intellectual stimulation. **There are 5 stages of remedying the writing skills** and empowering you with a great self-expression in writing. They are in tight connection with the same levels of developing any language habit and speech skill.

The levels of the writing skills are also the stages of learning to speak correctly, or the stages of managing the language **extemporaneously**. *(See Book One, "Second Language Consciousness")*. There are five levels of language mastery for you to empower. They are:

1. Random Writing - Micro-Level - This is the level of writing with no conscious control. That is the lowest level of speech mastery, when the brain is not controlled by the mind at all. As a matter of fact, it's not ready to be controlled by the mind because the mind is totally channeled by the native language. A speaker uses some words, phrases, or disconnected sentences in a foreign language. Through the entire book, we keep emphasizing **the importance of connectivity in the brain**. But language connectedness needs serious, conscious work and time

2. Framed Writing - Meta-Level - This is actually prepared writing, backed up by a written sample to refer to. Student' papers are framed by a teacher's instructions and the in-put. Such writing is normally well-outlined, but it is mostly of a narrative or descriptive nature. There is very little critical thinking in it. The writing skills are much more accurate grammatically

3. Channeled Writing - Mezzo-Level - This is the level at which good writing skills are displayed by a second language user. There is flexibility of self-expression and there is much less dependency on a written back-up text, found on the Internet or elsewhere. Writing may be well governed by **the conceptual vocabulary and the conceptual structure of thought in English.** Tight language control is needed because the form of the language is not in full lieu with the content yet. Much food for thought is needed to channel SL thinking.

4. **Conscious Writing - Macro-Level -** This is the level of very good writing skills. Writing is **accurate, consciously controlled, independent, governed by solid critical thinking and adequate self-expression.** Less language control is needed. The form and the content of the language are in synch.

5. **Masterful writing - Super Level -** Fluent, logical, coherent, extemporaneous self-expression. The second language mentality is established in the mind, thinking skills are solid and the language proficiency gets to the unconscious level of language use, close to that of a native language. **Language and speech are at the extemporaneous level.** Very little control is needed.

Space for Notes:

Writing develops a Thinking personality!

Chunk 5

Writing Strategies

Let's review the main strategies of writing that may be used separately or in complex with one another, depending on the thesis of your writing They are:

1. Narration = telling a story in writing or speech

2. Description = telling what something looks like

3. Illustration = giving examples and explaining

4. Comparisons - Contrast = looking for similarities and differences

5. Definition = explaining the meaning of something

6. Characterization = describing the character of somebody

7. Cause- Effect = telling the reason and the consequences of something happening

8. Argumentation = disagreeing or contesting what some one says in a formal, logical way

9. Persuasion = leading a person to believe or do s.t. by arguing or reasoning with them

10. Interpretation = deciding on the meaning of s.t. not very clear

These writing strategies define the type of academic essays that are normally written. They are:

1. A Narrative Essay

2. A Descriptive Essay

3. An Illustrative Essay

4. A Comparison- Contrast Essay

5. A Definition Essay

6. A Characterization Essay

7. A Cause-Effect Essay

8. An Argumentative Essay

9. A Persuasive Essay

10. An Interpretative Essay

Depending on the strategy of writing that you are using and the type of essay you are focusing on, you need to determine the right course of your writing action, putting mind over the brain. Be in charge of your brain. Don't let your being confused get reflected in your writing.

Don't Write on Inertia. Think before Writing!

English is Ruling the World!

You are Ruling Your English!

The Choreography

Of

Writing

Writing Techniques

Put the Emphasis on the Process of your Writing, Rather than its Result!

Remedy 1

Unblock Your Mind!

Remember, the best impromptu writing is the one that is well-prepared! Naturally, the starting point in writing is always a challenge to everyone. So, do not get confused with having a blank mind when you get yourself in front of the computer to write an essay, a business report, or anything of importance. Computers help us to find the information, to file it, to type it, to underline, to spell, to edit, to select, to copy, to correct, but they cannot help us think.

The thinking process is very individual, and it has to be monitored by a thinker him / herself. There is a big difference between us in cognitive ability. **Being sharp in thinking is the skill that has to be trained, too.** "Mental skills are trainable." (Scientific American mind", July, 2912)

Interestingly, the key to unlocking the initial block in the mind is language, for **language and thinking are inseparable.** So, the best way to become a sure writer is to read as much as you can. Reading gives food for though, so **reading should precede your writing.** When you read, you should observe the techniques and style of professional writers, Take note of how good writers organize their ideas, or how they express them. They may do it openly, or explicitly; they may also communicate their messages between the lines, or implicitly. Never start writing immediately, even when you are time restricted. So, to unblock your mind and focus on:

1. X-ray the reading materials for the food for thought. Fill yourself up with information, or inform yourself on the subject mater of your task in writing. You might want to research you it on the internet, print the information pertaining to your topic out, underline the most interesting ideas, write the thoughts that cross your mind while reading on the sides of the text, mark the sentences that might back your thoughts up as the quotations. Thus, you are giving the boost to your mind; you are feeding it food for thought.

2. Backing your mind up with the conceptually-loaded vocabulary that communicates the information that you singled out. Remember the rule: **Vocabulary shapes thinking!** Underline the word-combinations that you think are carrying the messages that you caught your aware attention. A native language speaker does not need the language back-up like that, but you definitely do. The conceptually-loaded word-combinations will channel your thinking when you start writing. *(See Remedy 9" Channeled Speaking, and Vocabulary Habits, Remedies 54,55,56)*

3. Finally, outlining you writing conceptually. Sort out the conceptual structure of your writing, its mental framework. Let it be only three ideas, to begin with. Write these ideas down and start furnishing them with the vocabulary unites that shape these thoughts. Organize the vocabulary nits conceptually, that is, according to the concepts that they communicate

Space for Notes:

Acquire mental Discipline!
Think before Writing!

Remedy 2

Conceptual Writing

Writing in based on **critical thinking skills** that are evolving while you are speaking or writing, Good writing requires your conscious attention to what you want to communicate to your readers. You absolutely need to take control of your brain while writing because **you are not your brain; you are the driver of your brain**. So, before you try to figure out what to write about, you must design the route of your writing / driving in the mind to channel your brain through it.

First, develop **the conceptual structure in your mind of the ultimate result of your writing, its thesis.** Keep it in mind that the work of any writer starts with the idea that gets shaped in the title of a book, a story, an article Then the process of **structuring and compartmentalizing** of the sorted out conceptual material begins. By compartmentalization, we mean the ability to break down the thinking process into concepts that you want to communicate through your writing.

Second, you need mental **food for thought** before you start writing any paper, be it an academic essay, a business report, or just a letter to a friend. A computer is an endless source of information that you need on any subject. Obviously, **reading is the first stage for writing** because it stimulates critical thinking skills and helps you generate new ideas in the brain. Be sure to learn **to read between the lines,** getting deep into the tapestry of the author's thinking and feeling. Generate your own ideas / argumentation as the result of such insightful reading.

Third, the next step is to cloak those ideas into appropriate vocabulary attire that channels your thinking conceptually, that is you need **to sort out the conceptually-loaded vocabulary.** Start writing out the vocabulary units that channel the concepts the author is communicating in the text, or the concept-prompting words that you are processing in your mind yourself while reading, or while just probing the subject mentally. **Organize these vocabulary units into one logical sequence,** the blueprint for your writing. Thus, you organize your thoughts into one conglomeration of concepts, backed up with the vocabulary units to express them in.

Forth, outline your writing in accordance with the conceptual structure that you have singled out in the form of **a conceptual plan.** Whatever the form of your writing is, it should have an introduction, body, and conclusion. Be sure to have **the thesis,** or the ultimate result vision of your writing presented at the end of your introduction, the specifics of the conceptual development of your wiring in its body part, and the position that you take as a writer on the issues presented in the conclusion. **Finally,** start writing with the outline in front of you.

Space for Notes:

"Language Shapes Thought"

Lera Boroditsky

Remedy 3

Channeled Writing

Writing may be reproductive, creative, business, or academically-bound. There different types of essays, too. But we are not going to get into that. There are many good books on writing that you might find helpful on the subject of academic, business, or creative writing,

Our focus is to help you make every type of writing **thoughtful, reflective, well-organized**, and written in accordance with the right language behavior. The basic idea of any off- the top of the head speaking or writing is the **mental structuring of** our "**impromptu creation.** In the previous remedy, in step four, we have mentioned the importance of the conceptually loaded vocabulary that leads you through your writing. Actually, the same technique is essential when you are preparing for your speaking, as is mentioned in *Remedy 9. "Channeled Speaking,"* Also, check out the example in *Remedy 56, Vocabulary Habits section.*

The vocabulary skills, associated with the conceptual reading, writing, speaking or, listening is the name of the game. You absolutely need to learn to single out **the conceptual vocabulary blueprint** for any of the language creative activity. So, channeled writing is in fact the writing channeled by the pivotal conceptual vocabulary. If we take the simplest topic "My Working Day," we can easily figure out the conceptual vocabulary blueprint to channel the writing on this topic later. Here you go;

1. to wake up 2. to stretch and yarn 3. to get up 4. to go to the bathroom 5. to wash the face and clean the teeth 6. to take a shower 7. to get dressed 8 to have a quick breakfast 9. to be in a hurry to work 10. to drive to work 11. It takes me. 15 min. to…12. to get to work on time 12. to start at 9 sharp 13. to have a lot of work to do 14. to have a break 15. to have lunch 16. to continue working 17. to be over at 6 pm. 18. to go home 19. to be stuck in the traffic 20 to come home at … Now, let's write a short paragraph, channeled by the word-combinations above. More practice is provided in the "Impeccable English" section.

My Working Day

I normally wake up at 7 o'clock in the morning. I stretch, yarn, and get up, ready for a new working day. First, I go to the bathroom, wash my face, clean my teeth, and take a shower. Then I get dressed and have a quick breakfast. After breakfast, I am in a hurry to work. I always drive to work. It takes me about a half hour to get to work on time. My working day starts at 9 sharp. I have a lot of work to do. Etc.

Space for Notes:

Zero in on the Conceptual Vocabulary

Blueprint!

Remedy 4

The Framework of Essay Writing

To begin with, there are many different types of essays that can be written for academic purposes. but we are not going to describe them. This information is available in numerous books on writing. We will focus here on **the general know-how** of the framework of essay writing that you can have at hand any time you need it. Once you have the topic for an essay to write, unblock your mind first, following the three steps that we suggest in **Remedy 1.** After figuring out what to write about, you must **develop the structure of your writing**, its outline on a piece of paper. Structure is like a strong force that guides the development of your thought. It channels your writing in the right direction. The structure of an academic essay always consists of the 3 main parts- **Introduction, Body, and Conclusion.**

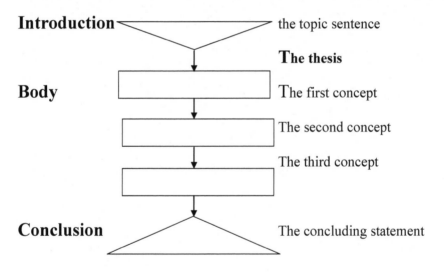

1. Visualize this design of an essay in your mind, and try to retrieve it each time you need to write an essay. Look carefully at the topic and see what it asks you to do.

2. Figure out the thesis of your writing, its communicative purpose, focusing it either on the information that you had accumulated on the topic, or your general outlook that you need to keep expanding through constant reading. Limit your thesis to the three major points / concepts that you want to communicate to your reader. Organize them conceptually and logically on a piece of paper. Leave some space between them for the word-combinations that will help you to word them out adequately.

3. Write down the conceptually-loaded vocabulary under each concept. It's your essay blueprint. Start writing, but first think then write! The native language might take the lead.

Space for Notes:

Don't Think and Write!

Constructing Your Writing

Now that you have prepared your mind for writing and have the outline for it in front of you, start constructing your writing. But stick to the Rule:

General ⇒ **Specific** ⇒ **General**

1. Your introduction should be general in meaning. It should contain no I pronouns, np examples, no stories of any kind. It should be a paragraph that presents the topic in a general, philosophical way. The introduction is for the reader to get into the subject of your writing, and for you to **intellectualize on its mental value.** a) To accomplish that, you need to **start writing with the topic sentence** that is directly connected to the topic in meaning. That is why it is called so. Chose the sentences of a general value, like;

1. There is a lot of talking about...

3. It is very important to mention that...

2. Generation ago, people...

4. The present day times are characterized with...

b) Precede writing with **2 to3 supporting statements** that back up your topic sentence.

c) Finish your introduction with **the thesis that introduces the three concepts** that you would like *to develop / back up / criticize,/ agree / disagree with / argue / persuade* your reader about.

2. The body part of your essay should be specific in its content, but the same in structure as the introduction. a) It should also start with the topic sentence of the paragraph that introduces your first concept, point, idea that you had sorted out as your first argument. b) Support the topic sentence of the first paragraph with details, examples, illustrations - **"the proof of the pudding.** Be specific, be argumentative, be persuasive, be overly intellectual about the point that you want to make. The same goes to the other two more paragraphs that you need to develop.

3. Finally, a successful writer must draw his / her comments together **in a strong, clear conclusion of a general type again.** To help you do that, we want you to start your conclusion with:

a) the expression of your personal opinion on the issues in question.

b) Give a reader advice on the subject matter, like: **We should**…

c) Express your hope to finish the essay on a positive note, like: **I hope we will** …

d) Wrap the essay up with the concluding statement that should be in lieu with the topic sentence or the topic itself. It may contain a good saying, a proverb, a line from a poem, just a smart thought to round doff the essay beautifully.

"The Choices we make dictate the Life we live!"

Remedy 6

X-Raying an Essay

When you finish your essay, you need to do a very important revision work on the two levels: **the level of content and the level of form.** *(See Section1, the Art of Writing, Chunk 3)* The questions below will help you focus on the main quality points in your essay's content and its form. Put the mind over the brain and **start editing or x-raying your essay holistically,** on both levels- its overall meaning and the grammatical accuracy. **Do self-assessment,** answering the questions below. Circle the "Yes / No" answers on the right and work on the negative responses later to better your essay both in terms of its content and the form.

X-Raying the Essay on the Level of the Content:

1. Introduction

a) Does the introduction to your essay have
the topic sentence?   Yes / No

b) Do you have 3 to 5 **supporting sentences**
after the topic sentence/?   Yes / No

c) Do you have **the thesis** at the end of your introduction?
Does it have any **three points of interest** to focus on/?   Yes / No

2. Body *(3 paragraphs)*

a) Do you have **the topic sentence of each paragraph**?   Yes / No

b) Do you develop each paragraph, providing
the proof for your concepts?
(examples, illustrations, consideration, etc.)?   Yes / No

c) Do you round off the paragraphs with **the**
concluding statement that
contains your position on the issues in question?   Yes / No

3. Conclusion

a) Do you express **opinion** on all the aspects of the topic?   Yes / No

b) Do you provide any **advice, solution of the problem** /s?   Yes/ No

c) Do you finish your essay **on the positive note?**   Yes / No

d) Do you round off your essay with an
interesting concluding statement?   Yes / No

X-Raying the Essay on the Level of the Form:

1. Do you follow the correct word-
order in English? (**S+ V+O+P+T**)   Yes / No

2. Do your sentences s vary in structure
(**Simple, Compound, and Complex**)?   Yes / No

3. Do you see any fragments (**unfinished sentences**)?   Yes / No

4. Are there any run- on sentences (**and..and…and)?**   Yes / No

5. Is there **logical connection** between sentences?   Yes / No

6. Do you use **thought connectors** between the
sentences and the paragraphs?   Yes / No

7. Do you detect any **unclear sentences** in the sense?   Yes / No

8. Do you feel you have some **direct translations**
form your native language?   Yes / No

9. Are you happy about **the vocabulary** you are using?   Yes / No

10. Are there any **spelling mistakes** in your essay?   Yes / No

11. Do you observe **the mechanics of writing**
(Commas, capitalization, periods)?   Yes / No

12. Do you use the correct **parts of speech**?	Yes / No
13. Do you detect any **subject-verb disagreement** in any sentence?	Yes / No
14. Are the **verb tenses** used accurately?	Yes / No
15. Do you use the **Passive Voice, Modals, Gerunds, and Conditionals** correctly?	Yes / No
16. Do you use your **articles** correctly?	Yes / No
17. Are you sure of your **preposition?**	Yes / No
18. **Are you happy with your writing altogether?**	Yes / No

Conscious Writing makes it Perfect!

Remedy 7

Use Thought - Connectors!

As we have mentioned many times throughout the book, the connection factor between the left and the right brains, between the language habits and the speech skills, between your thinking and your writing, between your speaking and writing is a determining prerequisite for the quality of your English to grow.

This factor is equally important in your writing. *(Check with the Speaking section, Remedy13)* So, be sure to connect the paragraphs in your essay and the sentences inside the paragraphs with **the thought - connectors and transitional phrases** they make your writing more coherent and readable. Take a look at the diagram of an essay structure in Remedy 4, the arrows between the paragraphs indicate the thought- connectors that have to be used in these places. **Note the use of a comma after the thought -connectors.**

Here are the most helpful ones, grouped, according to the purpose that you might have in mind:

1. To introduce your point:

a) There is no denying the fact that...

b) There has been a great deal of attention paid to...

c) There is a lot of controversy about...

d) It goes without saying that...

2. To support your idea:

a) Typically,

b) Remarkably,

c) Conversely,

d) Technically,

3. To explain your point:

a) The thing is,

b) The point is,

c) The problem is,

4. To strengthen the point:

a) Given all that,

b) Taking all that into consideration,

c) That's not to say that...

d) It translates into...

e) It is overstated / understated that...

5. To move to another point:

a) It is essential for sb. to...

b) It is paramount to comment on... ...

c) It is drastically important to....

d) It is crucial to point out that...

6. To express your attitude

a) Interestingly,

b) Personally,

7. To express doubt:

a) It's questionable if...

b) I am doubtful about...

c) I have some doubts as to...

d) We need to address the problem of...

e) It brings up the point of...

8. To agree with an idea

a) I totally agree with...

b) I cannot but agree with...

c) It makes sense to ...

d) It sounds interesting / convincing / reasonable /sensible

9. To disagree with somebody on something:

a) I cannot agree with the idea that

b) I totally disagree with...

c) It's pointless to say that...

d) It doesn't make sense to me that...

e) It's ridiculous to...

10. To provide examples:

a) For example,

b) For instance,

c) To illustrate,

d) I, for one, think that...

e)i can back up my idea with an example from...

11. To make an addition:

a) More than that,..

b) Moreover,

c) Also,

d) Other than that,

12. To compare / contrast

a) Likewise,

b) To compare,

c) In contrast,

13. To explain the cause

a) Since .../ Because...

b) Inasmuch as

14. To express concession:

a) Even though... / In spite of

b) Nonetheless, / Nevertheless,

15. To conclude the point:

a) So, / Therefore, / Thus,

b) In fact, / As a matter of fact,

16. To conclude the writing:

a) In sum, / In conclusion,

b) To conclude, / To summarize,

c) In a nutshell,

d) To sum it all up,

"A Little Organization goes a Long Way."

Remedy 8

Brain Writing

Brain writing is a writing activity that is generated without any prior preparation and requires immediate brain work on a mind-set. It's a great exercise to train your writing skill by spontaneous thinking. However, it is always a good idea to limit the number of sentences in which you present your amplification of a mind-set in question. Let's start with **5 sentences** of which one sentence goes to an Introduction, three sentences to the Body, and one sentence is supposed to wind up the Conclusion. Then, you might change the number of sentences to 7or 9.

"Life does not adjust to Us, We Adjust to Life!

1. To begin with, this is the statement that defines the essence of the philosophy of life.

2. No doubt, life is tough for every one, and it shapes us personally a lot.

3. Some of us get life-beaten, life smitten, or even life paralyzed due to the troubles that might be too bad to handle.

4. However, we should be stronger and face life challenges calmly to be abile to make quick decisions and resolve any problem that life might cast our way in the best way possible.

5. In a nutshell, my personal approach to life is: "Life is tough, but I am tougher!"

There are exactly 5 sentences in this brain writing, and they represent the introduction, the body, and the conclusion of your **spontaneous brain work on the topic**. Such brain writing teaches you to be in charge of every sentence in writing. It means that you might want to check with *Remedy 2, Grammar section.* Go over the types of sentences in English. This exercise trains you to stay away from non-stop writing in which there are endless use of the conjunction and in a non- stop way: **And... and...and...** Such sentences seem to be common for speaking, but, in fact, they are mental pollutants that disconnect the thoughts and mess up the thinking of the speaker / writer.

Obviously, disconnectedness is killing the thought! According to the rule of the right language behavior, you should establish a tight control over every sentence both in speaking and in writing. The thing is, non-stop speaking results into non-stop writing since speaking affects your writing in a direct way. Make your vocabulary the passport of your exceptional personality. Let it display your intellect to your advantage. Use the practice of brain writing to promote good writing habits. Let the mind-sets that are positioned at the bottom of every page of the book be the basis for your brain training. Be overly smart! **Write extemporaneously!**

Space for Notes:

From Muddled Thinking to Controlled Thinking!

Remedy 9

"Perception is More Important than Intent!"

Next, step out on the stage of your mind to practice your writing consciously. Your conscious intelligence is developed by writing, and it is properly working only on the mind's screen of full wakefulness and alertness. **The process of rationalizing your writing is the name of the technique.** Superficial writing needs to be changed into conscious, perceptive writing. It means that you need to keep in mind that some one is going to read your piece of writing and get the massage that you intend to communicate with it. But your intention to tell some one something depends totally on how you present your ideas for the reader to be able to perceive them correctly. So, the perception of the information that you communicate with your writing is much more important than the intention that you initially had. The problem is that if you are not **in charge of the form and the content** of your ideas; they might be perceived wrongly by your reader, if at all. A reader needs to digest your writing adequately, and the percentage of his/ her perception of what you write is your responsibility. That's what language literacy requires. Naturally, you have to make your writing **manageable and observe the language-speech integrity** in every sentence you write. Try to remedy your writing skills by following a simple ritual that we suggest below. A ritual is a ceremony your brain runs by.

Writing Ritual = Strategic Thinking

1 Stop and **think about the master message** *that you want to communicate with your writing.*

2. Structure your thoughts in paragraphs, **prioritizing them strategically** *for the coherence of the ideas that they express.* **Design each idea in your mind** *for the message it carries.*

3. **Sort out** *and jot down the* **word-combinations** *that might help you to frame those thoughts in the corresponding part that you are planning to develop into a paragraph later.*

*4. Start writing with **the aware attention on the texture of your writing** (the English word- order, the sentence structure, the logical connection between sentences, the tenses, the use of the articles, the precision of the chosen vocabulary, the punctuation, etc.)*

*5. Read each written sentence back to **X-ray its correctness** and then write the next one. **Check the flow of your ideas** for their logic and persuasion. Use thought-connectors.*

*7. Finally, conclude with **your position on the issue** outlined as the master message in your writing Take the position of a reader and see whether a reader's perception is adequate to your intent. Make changes, if need be. **Like yourself in doing that. Respect your mind!***

Space for Notes:

To Be Interesting, Get Interested!

Remedy 10

Mind-Sets as the Topics for Writing

Academic essays are normally written in response to topics. **We think that mind-sets serve the goal of developing the strategic thinking skills** in English much better than the topic that is normally used for academic writing purposes. They are more workable and effective for a writer's thinking critical skills because, on the one hand, they are not backed up by any predictable essay-writing on the Internet, and on the other, you do need to expand your own thinking skills to on the mind-set that are always thought-provoking.

I have been practicing such writing with my students for decades, and it has proven to be extremely productive in every respect

No plagiarism is possible here, and so, the academic worry of the instructors of writing is easily eliminated. Other than that, such writing integrates both language habits and speech skillsPlease note here that the transfer of the right language / grammar information does not occur instantaneously.

You need to utilize it continuously and religiously. All the learning strategies and objectives, presented in the book to remedy your language habits and speech skills will not work, unless you work on the correctness of your thinking, speaking and writing with conscious attention and persistence The ability to integrate thinking, speaking, and writing **needs** time to be shaped in your right brain that creates speech. We need **to convert the right thinking into the right speaking, and the right speaking into the right writing, that is to synthesize language and speech.** Working with the mind-sets is a great way to do it.it gives workable, not robotic results. So, mind-sets put a lot of strain on the brain and train you for free, mind-expanding writing. This activity may have the following form:

Free Speaking / Writing

The Mind-Set:

"The Choices we make Dictate the Life we Live".

Mind-Expanding Vocabulary Chart

Nouns:	Adjectives	Adverbs	Verbs	Word-Combinations
Option action etc.	numerous tough	decisively constantly	to opt to undertake	to make decisions to take action

Space for Notes:

Persistence Beats Resistance!

Remedy 11

Create the Bank of Ideas

We suggest that you accumulate the bank of ideas. Below, some of the mind-sets to start your **mental bank account**. When you see the mind-se, take a while to think to outline your thinking. It will enable your mind **to extemporize your thinking in a speaking or writing form**. *(See the book" Americanize Your Language, Emotionalize Your Speech "for more mind-sets and language management rules)*.

When we try to amplify a mind-set and elaborate on**, we engage mental processing action,** which includes sorting out the information, digesting it, organizing, and immediate problem solving. A writer becomes a creator in a true sense of this word. Speaking / writing on the mind-sets make your English **more emotionally manageable, too.** You can easily improvise on them.

See the key word from the mind-set on the left side of the list, and the mind-set on the right one. Take a piece of paper and close the part of the list with the mind-sets. Try to reproduce them by thr key word of left part of the list. They are very handy as the topic sentences of paragraphs for your essays, or they can serve excellently as the concluding statements to round off your essay in the conclusion. Keep depositing ideas, quoted into your bank. It's a great display of intelligence, too.

Enrich Your English!

Bank of Ideas:

1. Limits	*"The limits of your language is the Limits of your World".*
2 Education	*Education is a Progressive Discovery pf your own Ignorance.*
3. Teachable	*People live as long as they are Teachable.*
4. Tough	*Tough Times do not Last, Tough People Do!*
5. Treat	*"Treat the People as you want to be treated"*
6. Tougher	*Life is tough, but I am tougher!*
7. To be	*If it's to Be, it's up to Me!*
8. Friend	*Be your own Best friend!*

Sow a Thought, Reap an Action!

Remedy 12

Writing Dictations

Writing dictations is one of the most effective steps in developing writing strategies. Writing dictations is, in fact, language / speech enhancing work. It is a simple, yet very comprehensive approach because it has a synthesizing value. **You are working on your listening, thinking and writing skills n tandem.**

Writing dictations is language / speech activity of incredible potential It involves the interplay of mental visualization of the words heard and develops the brain's connectivity. Sense is governing the work, especially when you have to deal with the words that are look alike and the sound alike, or **homonyms.** *(See the Remedy on homonyms in the Listening Skills part below.)* E.g. **It's** hard to tell. - I have a smart phone. I like **its** sound.

Like a musician needs to write down the notes of a musical piece he / she hears to train his / her musical ear, a language learner wants to train his / her inner listening of the language, when the feeling and thinking come in synch. So, writing dictations is **a great intellectual stimulation.** Anything can serve as a dictation for you: a few paragraphs from a novel, story, a travel guide, a joke, a newspaper article, just anything. Take the joke below and ask some one to dictate it to you. Mind the spelling of the words, the punctuation, and the grammar.

Let's be Wise and Improvise

A Way Out

Mark Twain and a well-known American story teller Chauncey M. Depew were once invited to a dinner party. When it was time to make speeches, Mark Twain was asked to say a few words. He spoke for over a quarter of an hour and his speech as a great success.

Then it was Mr. Depew's turn to say something. He stood up and said, "Ladies and gentlemen, before this dinner, Mark Twain and I agreed to exchange speeches. He has just delivered my speech, and I thank you for the warm reception you gave it. I am sorry to say that I have lost the notes of Mark Twain's speech and I cannot remember what he was going to say" With these words, Mr. Depew sat down, and the guests had a good laugh.

2. Now, ask someone to dictate the two statements below. Write them down first, and then do some brain writing. Write a 10 sentence impromptu amplification of what they mean. Remember the rules: **Put the mind over the brain!" and "No Brain, never Mind"**

Space for Notes:

Expand Your Attention Span!

Remedy 13

Different Venues of Speaking / Writing

Finally, there is one more piece of advice to upgrade your speaking and writing. In the Brain Writing section *(See Remedy 8),* we referred to writing or saying the limited number of sentences to shape you minds in the right direction and to avoid pointless non-stop, uncontrolled speaking or writing.

You might want to say / write in the **1-3- 1** way *(See Remedy 8, Brain Writing)*, or write **3** for the sentences **Introduction, 6** for the **Body part,** and **3** for the **Conclusion**. Most importantly, stick to the correct sentence structure and do not speak / write in a non-stop way. Do your training of your writing skills along these lines:

Speaking / Writing Venues

1. Let's describe...	*9. Let's argue that ...*
2. Let's improvise	*10. Let's persuade that ...*
3. Let's elaborate on...	*11. Let's prove that...*
4. Let's expand on...	*12. Let's retrospect about...*
5. Let's amplify...	*13. Let's reflect on...*
6. Let's create a story about ...	*14. Let's infer that ...*
7. Let's exemplify...	*15. Let's deduce that...*
8. Let's illustrate...	*16. Let's conclude that ...*

Doing this work, you are **developing your writing awareness,** which incorporates your language awareness and your critical thinking skills, helping you to gradually form a peculiar **language mindfulness** that is the essential part of the method of the right behavior that we are upholding to throughout the entire book.

Working on the development of your thinking skills along the lines above, it is imperative to manage yourself and the language in you. Language management skills, like everything else in life have to be practiced and learnt. *(See the Language Management Rules" in my book "Americanize Your Language, Emotionalize Your Speech".)* Llearn the most difficult skill of all: **Do not verbalize / write everything that comes to your mind! Sort the thoughts out, then say / write them.**

Space for Notes:

Put some Strain on your Brain!

Remedy 14

Control every Writing Moment!

In both your speaking and writing, you need to remind yourself of some **dos and don'ts.** Follow the new ritual of language control that this book promotes. Also, stay away from the verbal polluters, such as the word **"like"**, for example, used endlessly as a substitute for real English. Do not stigmatize your speech with junk words! Writing is shaping your thinking personality. Always **have the URV** *(The Ultimate Result Vision)* **of** your writing in mind to channel your thoughts. Follow the ritual below for your reference.

The Ritual of the Right Language Behavior in Writing:

1. **Be in charge of yourself first!** The harder you are on yourself, the better is the result! Don't get out of your writing frequency. Don't get distracted by your cell phone, texting or any other electronic activity. **Shut them off for the time of your writing.**

2. **Be the manager of your English!** Come to Terms with the Language in You! **Don't write on momentum; first, think, and then write!** If you are commenting on any piece of writing, be sure to establish a mind-to mind contact with the author and channel your thinking in agreement/ disagreement with his/ her ideas.

3. Eradicate **the sporadic nature of writing.** Don't write just what comes to your mind, without any prior outlining of the message that you want to communicate. **Regulate your thought diarrhea.** Channel your thoughts according to the planned outline. **Do not let your writing slide to the automatic writing** with nothing to say and with many mistakes that pollute your English, to begin with.

4. **Be in charge of your English mentality.** Don't let it slide to your native language control. Follow the English word- order; observe the English sentence structure, the correct tenses, the use of the conceptual vocabulary, the punctuation, and the other mechanics of writing. **Repetition is the mother of learning!** *Check with us on the website any time you need.*

5. Have the mental language police on the non-stop duty in your mind! Correct your mistakes then and there. Control your language habits and speech skills in unity; put your brain and mind together. **Strategize your speaking and writing with the ultimate result vision.**

6. Keep your eye on the ultimate goal - the best writing you! Writing is the passport of your mind! What your reader perceives, reading your piece of writing

Space for Notes:

Turn on your Brain Radar to Correct English!

Remedy 15

Focus on the Outcome

Finally, any work that you start in English, be it speaking, reading, writing or listening, you need to have **the URV of your work**, that is its **Ultimate Result Vision,** the necessity of having which we point out to you in Part 1., Section2 *(The Hierarchy of Our Goals)* Let us remind you here that speaking becomes much more controlled language-wise if you have the vision of the ultimate result of your speaking in mind. **The URV helps to stabilize your emotional brain,** your emotional intelligencer and it develops your emotional personality. Your Goal is Manageable Grammar! So, Have the Ultimate Result Vision of your language / speech transformation thanks to your speaking / writing all the time. The greatest axiom of life:

To have more than you've got, become more than you are!

Let's check what you've become having finished the work on the essential skills fin adult language learn- writing. Remember, adults start their language learning with writing down the new words, phrases, then visualizing then, reading them out loud, saying the, listening to them said, and finally internalizing them. **So, writing is the prerequisite of language leaning.** Please, test yourself on some new tips in managing your writing that we were trying to help you realize. Let's break down the information that you had to digest so far into some outcome questions for you to check yourself;

What did you come to know…?

1. What level of the writing skills are you in your assessment now? *(Chunk 3)*

2. Why do we write the way we speak? *(Chunk 1)*

3. How do you need to adjust the train of your thought in writing in English? *(Chunk 2)*

4. What do we mean by putting the form and the content of your writing in synch? *(Chunks 5,6)*

5. What doe conceptual (brain) writing mean? *(Remedies2,8)*

6. How are you supposed to construct your essay-writing? *(Remedies 4,5,6,7)*

7. How does vocabulary shape your thinking? What is channeled writing all about? *(Remedies 3.10.11)*

Don't write, without thinking first! And don't write on the automatic pilot!

Space for Notes:

Manage your Mind in Writing!

Remedy 16

Psychological Corner
(Building up Personal Stamina)

Ending up the remedial work on the writing skills, we need to rekindle the entire system of language / speech development in order **to maximize the effectiveness of the correct language behavior.** Though out the book, we were boosting your personal stamina to drive your language remedial work and help you manage your language better. Below, again have the mind formula that will boost you success in language learning, and, actually, in everything in life

"I am a strong, confident, and consistent master of my writing.

I can…

I want to…

I will…!

I am becoming better and better in my writing each time I need to write something.

I am on my quest of being the best!

When you become emotionally tuned in, your mind opens up for new knowledge and new accomplishment. We do not evolve to the next level unless we made the necessary changes in our thought processes. The same mental program will back you up, both emotionally and psychologically, in your work at the pronunciation, in figuring out of the grammatical structure of English that we present next, or in the expansion of your vocabulary that is forming up your thinking in English. You can practically apply it to anything. Just keep saying to yourself these magic words: **I can…; I want to …; I will…!.**

Self-boosters are a great way to give your psyche a back- up and your brain an emotional energizer. You need to help yourself emotionally to master a foreign language. Emotional intelligence is needed here. **The**

method of the Conscious Language Behavior is, actually, building the living intelligence in the language. By living intelligence we mean the state of deep consciousness and mental clarity in the language. You will step out of your relative, mechanical, emotional hullabaloo, knowledge of the language and start enjoying the conscious, operative, and optimal state of your language / speech competence.

Space for Notes:

Don't Wish it were Easier,
Wish you were better!"

Remedy 17

Language Speech Profile # 5

With the completion of this part of the book, we want you to walk out of your past Second language history with a sense of accomplishment. It is fundamental to your understanding of your **self-concept in English.** You have a better idea of the road map that you will continue following to the quality English. It is a controlled, action-filled, rational strp in your English life. You are much more conscious of what you are rising to in the language. You are learning to listen, speak, read, and write with a **constant control over your English.**

Self-Assessment

*1. I have a better idea now of **the main trouble spots in my writing.***

*2. I you have managed **to reason out the main directions** to remedy my writing.*

*3. **I am more conscious of my language errors** while writing and I feel very good when I see them and correct them then and there. I do not let my language **slide to the automatic writing** with many uncorrected mistakes that pollute my English.*

*4. I enjoy writing because I develop my strategic thinking with it a lot. I am doing great! **I continue the quest of being the best1***

Now, do the rating of your Language Habits and Speech Skills **on the scale of 1 to 10**

Language Habits

1. Pronunciation Habits -

2. Grammatical Habits -

3. Vocabulary Habits -

Speech Skills

1. Listening Skills -

2. Speaking Skills -

3. Reading Skills -

4. Writing Skills -

Space for Notes:

"Opportunity Follows Difficulty!"

Donald Trump

End of Part 2 "Remedy Your Writing Skills'

English is Ruling the World!

You are Ruling Your English!

Part 3
Speech Odyssey / Reading Skills

Remedy
Your
Reading Skills

Reading Changes your Intellectual Landscape!

English is Ruling the World!

You are Ruling Your English!

Section 1

The Art
Of
Reading

Information for Consideration

Knowledge is more than Words
on the Page!

Chunk 1

Food for Thought

Instructional Poem

We need

    A lot

Food for

    Thought

              To analyze and to ref-

                lect

              To consider and to pro-

                ject!

But our brain stomachs develop an inflam-

    mation

From the clutter of digital infor-

    mation

              How do we get on a

              Diet

              Of a good, sorted out

              Mind,

The mind that can de-

    lete

The redundant info-

    Shit,

The mind that will
Store
Only the needed
Info

Are there any pills or
Meals
To obtain the brain of the best
Deals?

Yes, I say, there is a solution
For the human mind's evolution!

Discipline it and keep it
Clean
Before it becomes ob-
scene!

Also, say what you
Mean
And mean what you
Say

To be totally
Clear
At the social
Bay!

But try not to

Smear

The right brain's hemis-
phere

Learn to systematize and to re-
vise,

Don not constantly ana-
lize!

Also, don't let your brain become a

Zone

For a dirty electronic

Phone,

Use it rationally and to the purpose

To be always in the mental focus!

Finally, do not forget to cut your

Talk,

Better walk, walk, and

Walk

Exercise and read

A lot

To have more foods for

Thought!

Chunk 2

Brain Talk

Reading is an active thinking process. It **develops a higher conscious mind,** the part of the brain that is called the wise and knowing mind. This is what we are after when we are talking about remedying your reading skills through the practices that we offer to your attention here. It's an accepted fact that reading develops intelligence, creativity, and super intelligence, but it needs proper self-control.

When you are reading, you absolutely need to control the power of your mental focus, or your **aware attention to the conceptual structure of the text.** Focused reading helps you keep open higher and more efficient brain processes. Conscious thought remains uninterrupted and much greater level of intelligence is the result. **By reading with aware attention and sorting out the information that you need**, you distinguish between the front lobes brain behavior and the hard drive reptilian back lobes behavior, which is in charge of our automatic responses to the incoming information. Automatic reading is never conscious.

The same way as you are teaching yourself to be in control of your automatic speaking or writing, you need to **develop the skill for conscious reading.** Humans have an unlimited capacity to learn. Unlike computer, no human brain can ever say" Hard drive is full" We are using only a fraction of our brain potential. With practice, the front lobes of your brain will scan any thought for its relevance to your channeled thinking; your reading will become resultfully beneficial both for your speaking and writing.

All you need to do is X-ray the reading for food for thought. You must be able to disseminate between frontal lobes intelligence and reptile brain, not thinking reaction. Go against conventional wisdom and the status quo of knowing nothing about **proper brain self-control.** There is so much material on the Internet for you to feed on, but you need to work with it creatively, the same as you have to be picky in what you chose to eat.

The brain is like a muscle. When you use it consciously, your mind produces result. The brain is a complex rational computing machine. Survey your left brain skill for the structure of your reading and your right brain for its content and try to operate them in synch, consciously. Reading in this way develops your aware attention and balanced brain power.

Finally, learn to be quiet while reading. **Expand your consciousness**. Think beyond regular practice of automatic reading. **Stay language aware!** Receive intuitive signals from your brain for the value of the material in front of your eyes. Jot the ideas that you generate down in the conceptual vocabulary way. It is the blue print of your own thinking that you will develop on the basis of this vocabulary in your verbal interaction or written one.

Space for Notes:

Structure your Thinking through Reading!

Chunk 3

Reading and Conceptualizing

The crucial skill to be developed in reading is the skill to synthesize and **generalize the information, or to conceptualize it.** We need to learn how to filter the text in the mind, sorting out the incoming information and organizing it into the meaningful blocks that communicate **the master message** to us, normally coded in the title of the article, a book, a report, or a simple note. We call such technique - **conceptualizing.**

The brain has a remarkable ability to analyze the information, process it and guide it. You need to learn how to manipulate the ideas that you get while reading and form them into **the conceptual hierarchy.** This is a special skill of molding the reading process into the mental one.

You need to learn to read between the lines, the skill that you most certainly have in your native language. But you need to connect the understanding through **thinking and feeling together.** Thanks to this link, the brain will orchestrate the final accords - **the concept of the text.** The initial idea crystallizes and gets outlined and shaped in your mind. It's your primary notion of the whole.

By contextualizing the information, or **breaking it down into concepts**, you develop the ability to organize the whole text or separate paragraphs of the text into a set of meaningful messages that the author of the text communicates to the readers. Thus, you will get the conceptual structure of the text, the logical pattern of ideas that the author imposes on us.

Write the concepts that you have extracted from the text down, especially if you need this information for an essay, a business report or a talk. Make the conceptual structure of the text, or its **mental skeleton.** The whole body of the text that you are reading becomes very easy to digest. You get into the writing laboratory of n author of the text, his / her **conceptual framework.**

Conceptual Structure of a Text =
The Mental Framework of an Author

To be able to do that, you do not need to read absolutely every sentence in some pretty challenging texts that are hard to crack intellectually even for some native language readers. We mean scientific texts, sophisticated business reports, or any information-loaded texts. All you need to master is **to do speed reading**. The most important information is enclosed in the topic sentence of the text, or a paragraph, and in the concluding statement either of the whole text or a paragraph. Working on developing your **conceptual skills** through reading, you become more confident in your reading that will get considerably stronger though such practice.

Space for Notes:

Reading develops a Thinking Personality!

Chunk 4

Reading Critically

Reading critically is reading for ideas, or conceptual reading, as opposed to superficial reading. To maximize the effectiveness of reading, you should learn to read critically. No doubt, you read critically in your native language, trying to extract real meaning of the written text that is hidden between the lines. Such reading is always conscious and very fulfilling. That is why, **the ability to read the text incisively** is so important when we read something in a foreign language

The initial stage of superficial reading just for the content flow has to give way to deep, conscious penetration into the text that provides food for thought and fills your right brain up with the new vocabulary units and a new intuitive feeling of the language.

Conceptual reading opens a new dimension in the brain. Don't read mechanically or automatically, with only 30%., 20%, or even 10 % of the text being processed in the brain. **Read with aware attention**, knowing what information you are looking for in the text and therefore are downloading into your brain. Such reading is always charged with thought. **Such reading is conceptually- charged!**

It must be stressed here that there is a direct connection between conceptual writing and conceptual reading. Check with the *Remedy 2* in the Writing Section. It teaches you to start writing an essay, a paragraph, or even a small note with the topic sentence and finish your writing of any sort with the concluding statement.

These two sentences carry the main conceptual information in the text, a paragraph, a business report, or a note. Reading has the same strategies, especially if it is not junk reading that has populated our book stores. But we are talking here about quality reading that classically goes with the structure

General $\Longrightarrow$ **Specific** $\Longrightarrow$ **General**

Conceptual reading in this framework **develops your critical thinking skills and, therefore, is forming your English language consciousness**. We mean here that any active thinking while reading is very beneficial for a foreign language mental enrichment Reading conceptually, you are doing active reading as apposed to the passive reading when your mind is just sliding across the pages mindlessly, picking up the most interesting twists in the plot of the story or noodling around the pages in a relaxed search for something to catch your attention. For that matter, try to read as many thought- provoking books as possible.

Space for Notes:

Feel the Reward of Advanced Thinking!

Section 2

The Architecture Of Reading

Reading Strategies

Be Hungry for Knowledge!

Remedy 1

Proactive Reading

Throughout the book, we have been talking about conscious work at the language habits and speech skills. We have also noted how important conscious reading is for the second language This remedy is meant to give some workable tips for conscious reading. Conscious reading may be passive, active, and proactive.

Passive Reading $\Longrightarrow$ **Active Reading** $\Longrightarrow$ **Proactive Reading**

Passive reading is superficial and unconscious. **Active reading** is the reading with a purpose, the reading that helps you draw conclusions and form opinions, **Proactive reading** is totally conscious reading, and the reading that is also **linguistically aware**. Aware reading is the main mechanism of proactive reading in a foreign / second language.

First, to adequately understand a foreign text, pay aware attention to the inner beauty of the language in it. Unfortunately, many people lack this ability even in their native language, and it's a real shame. As a matter of fact, your reading comprehension depends on the level of your **being informed in the language linguistically.**

It also requires paying aware attention to the word- order in a sentence, and writing out the new words correctly. Focus on

a) **considering the context** they are used in and

b) **paying attention** to the part of speech that they are used in.

c) **never writing** out the translation of the new words mindlessly, without considering these two things that develop **your aware attention.** Reading proactively, you are conscious of the fact that the context may determine the part of speech of this or that word in the text. You are also fully aware of

d) the display of words that you need to word out your opinion in.

If you read proactively, the vocabulary that you use to frame out your ides becomes **workable verbally.** Alert your attention to the concepts these vocabulary units communicate. Remember, words generate thoughts. *(See Book Two, "Remedy Vocabulary Habits")*

Second, besides paying aware attention to the linguistic display of the text, you **get a better idea of its conceptual value,** which we refer to above. Here, you absolutely need to draw a parallel between the **classic structure of both good writing and reading.** Read the first sentence in each paragraph. It introduces the subject of the text, in the same way as the topic sentence of an essay introduces the point of your writing. Read the last sentence of a paragraph. The meat of each paragraph contains the proof of what it illustrates, exemplifies, or just intellectualizes on. Pay attention to the things that **resonate with you mentally and emotionally.** Finally, try to connect the language and the speech aspects together.

Space for Notes:

Be Immune to Linguistic Blindness in Reading!

Remedy 2

Vocabulary Channeled Reading

In Part Two, section 'Vocabulary Habits', we are instructing you how to process your new vocabulary through the parts of speech. Since reading is the greatest source of vocabulary, write out the new vocabulary units consciously, processing each vocabulary unit of interest through different parts of speech. **The vocabulary grid below teaches you how to process vocabulary in the brain.** This work will considerable enrich your vocabulary stock, and it will channel your thinking toward conceptual reading, that develops your **reasoning skills,** or thinking critical skills.

Vocabulary Processing Grid

Nouns Who? What?	Adjectives What kind Of...?	Adverbs How? Adj.+ ly	Verb In the Inf. form	Word-Combinations Blocks of vocabulary in the Infinitive Form
mind	mindful	mindfully	To mind	To be mindful about st.
interest	Interesting	interestingly	To interest	To be (get) interested in...
surprise	surprising	surprisingly	To surprise	To be (get) surprised with...
success	successful	successfully	To succeed	To be a success in...
pleasure	pleasant	pleasantly	To pleasure	To be pleasurable
impression	impressive	impressively	To impress	To make an impression on
information	informative	informatively	To inform	To be informed about
depression	depressive	depressively	To depress	To be depressing/ depressed
access	accessible	accessibly	To access	To have (get) an access to...
availability	available	availably	To avail	To be available for...

Discipline your Vocabulary in the Brain!

Remedy 3

Mind the Inversion!

We have noted above how much your understanding of what you read depends on how well you process the language structure and how good your vocabulary skills. You will be better able to grasp the meaning of the information if you are aware of another phenomenon in the English language that affects correct understanding of the read text.

This amazing phenomenon is called **inversion**. It is connected with the ability of the language to change one part of speech into another just changing the position of a word in a sentence. Since the English word-order is a "one-way street "(S + V+ O), **English words can function as different parts of speech,** depending on the position a word takes in a sentence and what it's meaning is in a particular context. E g. **But me no buts** *(a verb + a noun / a conjunction)*

In *Part Two, Remedy 53,* we comment on the importance of being familiar with this peculiarity of the English language. It is, of course, extremely important for you to keep it in mind while reading because this linguistic phenomenon is widely used in English.

Here are some examples:

1. A man decided **to desert** his hut in **the desert.** *(a verb; a noun)*

2. She **distinguished** herself from other rich and **distinguished** women in the society. *(a verb; an adjective)*

3. There was no **envy** in her for her sister, but she **envied** her friend for her better looks. *(a noun; a verb)*

4. A doctor listened to his **patient** with a **patient** attention. *(a noun; an adjective)*

5. You always **surprise** me with your **surprise** parties and all kinds of other **surprises.** *(a verb, ; an adjective; a noun)*

6. Since there is no time like the **present**, he decided **to present** her with **the present** right away. *(a noun; a verb, a noun)*

Mind you that the inverted nouns and verbs are accentuated differently. **Try to be mindful of the cases of inversion while reading.** Enrich your English with this skill.

Space for Notes:

"Every Word has a Different Power."

Yvonne Oswald

The Texture of Reading

To develop your reading skills, you also need to learn how **to X-ray the text for its texture-** its **vocabulary, its composition, and the conceptual structure** that it is built on. Your proactive reading will result in much better understanding of the conceptual messages in the text that the author of it communicates to us.

You will not feel trapped by the text if you read proactively; paying aware attention to the words those concepts are cloaked in. Vocabulary shapes thought. Precision of words is extremely important in writing.

That is why Mark Twain once wrote: **"The difference between just words and the exact words is the same as the difference between the lightning and a lightning bug"**. Every good author works on the precision of the words with which he communicates his / her message.

In the section *Vocabulary Skills, Remedy 52,* we teach you to process the unknown words through the parts of speech. Such vocabulary work will enrich your capacity of understanding any reading, and it will make your reading in English really knowledgeable and informative. It is one of the ways to make your vocabulary stock grow. **Conceptual Vocabulary is the Texture of Reading.**

Another way to enrich your mind is working with the conceptually- loaded vocabulary. You need to develop the ability to single out the vocabulary units that constitutes **the conceptual blue print of the text** that you are reading for whatever purpose. You might want to start with **the master message** that you reasoned out from the entire text first on a piece of paper. Do it by, generalizing on the information in the text, reading the author's message between the lines. Then you need to see how the master message that is normally directly connected to the title of the texts gets broken down into **minor messages** that each part of the text conveys.

Having worked on the entire text conceptually, you will have a **conceptual structure of the text** to back up on. It will be **the conceptual outline** of the text. Next, sort out the word-combinations that carry the conceptual meaning of this or that part of the text. This word-combination will constitute the **conceptual blueprint of the text.** So, shifting the gears of your aware attention from the minor details in the text, you train your brain to be more perceptive of the bigger ideas that give you food for though. This vocabulary blueprint of the text will channel your mind in speaking or writing on the topic in question; it will give you linguistic confidence, more language accuracy, and a needed precision of self-expression. **Conceptual vocabulary is the texture of every good piece of writing.** So, every good piece of writing has a conceptual structure that you need to X-ray and jot down in the way suggested above.

Space for Notes:

Explore Your Reading Vocabulary-Wise!

Remedy 5

Creative Reading

Alongside with paying aware attention to the vocabulary framework of a piece of reading, it is very important to do some brain work on it, or do the proactive reading in a three way fashion;

Synthesis $\Longrightarrow$ **Analysis** $\Longrightarrow$ **Synthesis**

General $\longrightarrow$ Specific $\longrightarrow$ General

Start thinking about a piece of literature, a story, a novel, a piece of poetry, or a business report in general terms first, evaluating the conceptual value or a contribution of a read piece into your intelligence. See how much food for thought you have gotten, having read that piece, if at all.

At the first Synthesis Stage we can:

1. **Perceive** the problem / idea that touched us

2. **Question** it or **probe the text** for it

3. **Claim our agreement/ disagreement** with the author

4. **Conceptualize** on the content, in a thesis like way

At the Analysis Stage we can;

1. Analyze

2. Amplify

3. Interpret	*6. Illustrate*	*9. Agree / disagree*
4. Prove	*7. Narrate*	*10. Argue*
5. Exemplify	*8. Describe*	*11. Criticize*

12. Express your own point of view	14. State your opinion	At the final Synthesis Stage we can:
	15. Give the position	
13. Express your point of view		

1. *Conclude*   2. *Assume*   3. *Infer*

4. *Express hope*   5. *Make generalizations*

6. *Discuss the effect of the catharsis*, *if any, on us*

Space for Notes:

Reading is Expanding your Mental Outreach!

Remedy 6

Inductive-Deductive Reading

As we have indicated in the *Chunks 2 and 3* of this part of the book, conceptual reading demands a lot of analysis *(inductive reading)* and generalization *(deductive reading)* on your part.

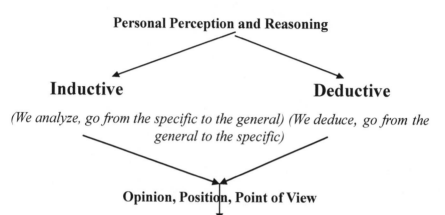

Personal Perception and Reasoning

Inductive   **Deductive**

(We analyze, go from the specific to the general) (We deduce, go from the general to the specific)

Opinion, Position, Point of View

Catharsis (Our Reasoning + Feeling after reading)

The art of reading starts with the X-raying of the story for its **compositional structure**. As a matter of fact, every classic piece of literature has a classic composition, like a good classic piece of music with its introduction, development of the theme and its final concluding accords Exploring the ways to develop the ESL reading skills in conceptual terms, we can actually see the two venues for post-reading activities:

Simple Reading	Conceptualized Reading
(Inductive skills are being developed)	*(Deductive skills are being developed)*
It is focused on the abilities of a reader	It is focused on the abilities of a reader
to narrate, to describe, to connect, and	**to generalize, to summarize, to assume, to conclude, to retell to infer**

Every piece of classic fiction contains a deep message that the author of a story, a novel, a piece of poetry wants to communicate to the readers. This message is usually coded in the title of a piece. It can also be broken down into minor messages in the chapter of the book and its main parts.

Space for Notes:

Read Insightfully for Ideas!

Remedy 7

Probe the Composition of the Text

Every classically written story and a novel have the composition that you need to detect to be able to **interpret any piece of literature insightfully**. Probing any well-written piece of literature for its composition, you can find in it:

1. Introduction

2 The starting moment

3. The thickening of the plot

4. The positive culminating points of the story / novel

5. The further development of the plot

6 The negative culminating point

6. The relaxation of the plot

7 The resolution of the conflict. *(A reader experiences **the catharsis**, a mental and emotional revelation, a deep, insightful, life changing cleansing if thought and feeling)*

To illustrate, let's take a close look at a well-known classic story **"Necklace" by Guy de Maupassant** that you can find in the book 'The International Story' by Ruth Spack or on the Internet The story "The Necklace", as any other classic piece of writing, amazingly resonates with the life nowadays in terms of the aspirations for a care-free life that some people have. We see what happens to people when material values blind them. It's a very engaging story. It has a lot of thought-provocative concepts that keep readers on toes to the end of the story.

We will X-ray the story for its conceptual structure or **conceptual hierarchy.** Then we'll extract **the conceptual vocabulary blueprint** with the help of which the author gets his ideas across to us. Try to get the story and read it. Have it in front of your for the conceptual analysis that is presented in the next remedy. This story will serve as a great example how to interpret a piece of fiction, how to examine it for its compositional structure, and how to pick the **conceptually loaded vocabulary** that can help you in the discussion of any story or in writing a paper on it. As any classic piece of literature, this story has a transparent compositional structure, and it is written in an extremely beautiful and precise language. So, try to constantly analyze your reading to become more a insightful reader.

Space for Notes:

The composition of a text has
a communicative power.

Remedy 8

The Conceptual Hierarchy of the Story "Necklace"

The composition of the story "The Necklace", its conceptual messages of the story, as well as its conceptual vocabulary blueprint are presented below. Learn how to interpret a structured story.

The Introduction

Concept # 1 - A pretty woman often considers her marriage "to be a mistake of nature."

1. To be a pretty and charming girl

2. To expect to be wedded by any rich and distinguished man

3. To be married to a little clerk at the Ministry of public Instructions

4. To dress plainly

*5. **To be unhappy as though she had really fallen from her proper station***

6. To suffer ceaselessly from the wretchedness of her life

*7. **To dream of dainty dinners and shining silverware***

8. To have no dresses, no jewels, nothing

*9. **To love nothing but that***

10. To like to be envied, to be charming, to be sought after

The Starting Point in the Story

Concept # 2 - Life casts us chances that we blindly do not appreciate

1. To return home with a triumphant air (M. Loisel)

2. To request the honor of M. and Mme. Loisel's company

*3. **To throw the invitation with disdain (Mme. Loisel)***

4. To have nothing to put on her back

5. To be not properly equipped

6. To be in despair (M. Loisel)

The Thickening of the Plot

Concept 3 - Being discontent with what you have ruins your life

1. To find the money to buy a pretty dress

2. To be still sad, uneasy, anxious, discontent

*3. **Not to have a single jewel***

4. To suggest wearing natural flowers

5. To be not convinced

6. To come up with an idea to borrow some jewels

Concept 4 - Being content with little is rarely a virtue.

1. To take out a large jewel box

2. To see precious stones of admirable workmanship

3. Not to make up her mind

4. To strive for more

5. To see a superb necklace of diamonds

6. To tremble at the sight of it

7. To flee with her treasure

The Positive Culminating Point in the Story

Concept 5 - Complete victory happens at a cost.

1. To make a great success

2. To be elegant, gracious, smiling, crazy with joy

3. To forget all in the triumph of her beauty

Concept 6 - Reality hits, anyway.

1. To be over at 4 o'clock in the morning

2. To bring her the modest wraps of common life

3. To want to escape so as not to be remarked by the other women

4. To walk home in despair

*5. **"All was ended for her!"***

The Negative Culminating Point of the story

Concept 7 - There is a pay off for every wrong doing in life.

1. To utter a cry

*2. **To have no necklace around her neck***

*3. **To be thunderstruck***

4. To be overwhelmed

5. To find nothing

6. To lose all hope

7. To go from jeweler to jeweler

8. To search for a replacement with chagrin and anguish

9. **To find one worth forty thousand francs**

10. To make a bargain for thirty four thousand francs

11. To take loans

12. ***To take up ruinous obligations***

13. ***To compromise all the rest of his life (M. Loisel)***

The Relaxation of the Plot

Concept # 8 - Honesty is always the best way for a resolution of a conflict.

1. To return the necklace

2. Not to open the case

3. Not to tell Mme. Forestier the truth

4. To fear to be taken for a thief

Concept 9 - "How Life is Strange and Changeful!"

1. To have a horrible existence

2. ***To work hard to pay off the dreadful debt***

3. To come to know privation

4. To be dressed like a woman of the people

5. To live a miserable life

6. And this life lasted for ten years.

7. To pay everything

8. To look old, hard and rough

The Catharsis

Concept 10 - "How little a thing is needed for us to be lost or to be saved!"

1. To take a walk

2. To perceive a woman with a child

3. To be still young and beautiful (Mme. Forestier)

4. To feel moved by her words

5. To tell her all about it

6. To be astonished beyond words

*7. **"You must be mistaken."***

8. "How you have changed!"

*9. **"That because of you!"***

10. To be proud and naïve at once

11. To be paste

*12. **"It was worth at most five hundred francs"***

Learn to Read Conceptually!

Remedy 9

Post Reading Steps

Above, we have demonstrated how to probe a story, a novel, a piece of good poetry. Let's go over the main steps. A very important point to note here is that **information flows down the conceptual hierarchy of any piece of reading as well as up**, that is from the conceptual hierarchy, back to the title of the piece of reading that carries the massage of the author in a condensed way. Below are the summarizing tips to follow that flow.

Probing a Piece of Literature

*1. Think about the content in terms of its **compositional structure***

*2. Probe the text for **the concepts that it carries**, implicitly (directly) or explicitly.(indirectly).*

*3. Pick and underline **the conceptually loaded words and word-combinations***

*4. Focus on interesting, **thought-provoking quotes**. Write them out. The author talks directly to you! The rest of the messages that the author communicates to you could be read between the lines. Master the skill of **reading implicitly**, getting into the most insightful messages in the text.*

*5. Write an **outline of the story** in the way we have presented above. In case of a novel, probe it for its compositional structure first and then see how the chapters of the novel come together to **communicate the concepts, the messages that the author gets across to us.***

*6. Write a response, synopsis, or an essay on the story, novel, a piece of poetry, if necessary, **channeling your writing by the conceptual outline** that you have prepared. (Check with the Remedy 3, Channeled Writing', Section 2. Writing Techniques) Use the conceptual outline as the plan for your verbal presentation, too.*

*7. **Develop the ability to discover meaning;** decipher **the** understatements between the lines of a text. Get the implied information in the text. **Learn to conceptualize it!***

*8. Deepen your ability to respond to literature emotionally and mentally. Always **reason out the cathartic effect** that any good reading has upon you. Such reading in English will expand your outlook immensely and will strengthen your psychological framework.*

*9. Finish any mentally challenging work with literature with your own position on the issues discussed. See how any intellectually-charged reading resonates with you. **Develop the right brain ability to synthesize and generalize** the received information.*

Space for Notes:

Learn to Make Generalizations while Reading!

Remedy 10

The Art of Reading = the Art of Thinking!

Finishing our overview of the Reading Skills, we deem it necessary to remind you that reading in English opens many cultural doors for you, widening your **cultural intelligence**, so essential in the new, globalized world.

Participating in a meaningful communication is a great skill. It can easily be developed now through the social network on the Internet. **Your input into the discussion needs to be specific, argumentative, and convincing.** Such communication necessitates letting go of wrong English and focusing on language- mindful responses that only your extensive reading and vocabulary accumulating can help you with.

Nothing hinders your progress more than closed mindedness and linguistic ignorance, be it reading, speaking, writing or listening. In fact, as you perceive the word display in reading, such is your real knowledge of the language and such is your vision of the world. Good reading enthuses us and inspires to be better. It teaches us to trace the logic of an author's thinking and appreciate its instructive messages.

All we have to do is to learn to read those messages between the lines inductively or deductively, analytically or systemically.

Most importantly, developing your reading skills consciously will help you transform your language habits into the speech skills much more resultfully. **Reading can refine your language / speech self-presentation because it creates your mind!**

Finally, your thinking brain, your neocortex, is a "virgin territory" *(Ray Kurzweil)* when a new mentality is created on it. "It has the capacity of learning and therefore creating connections between the pattern recognizers *(prior knowledge recognizers)*, but it gains those connections from experience."

Obviously, the more you read, the more connections you establish in your neocortex, and therefore more intelligent you become in the second language."The neocortex is continuously trying to make sense of the input presented in it. It helps to direct your thinking." *Ray Kurzweil calls such process "directed thinking."*

We call it **channeled reading, writing, speaking, or listening,** as it is commented on above. See these sections in the book for your reference. They systematize your basic speech skills and remedy them systemically

Space for Notes:

"Words Change the DNA of Thought!"

Yvonne Oswald

Remedy 11

Must Haves

Finishing our remedial work at the reading skills, we need to remind you that this work has to be disciplined as much as anything, if not more. Reading is the main source of information, and together with writing, it develops your critical thinking skills in English a lot. Therefore, we suggest that you have the following **four sub-parts in the section "Reading"** of your notebook.

Part 1 - **Operative Vocabulary**

Reading any piece of literature, write out **the new words that carry the conceptual information** and are important for the understanding of the plot of the story / novel, or the subject matter of an article, a report etc. **Be sure to indicate the part of speech** that every new word belongs to. (*Check out Remedy 57 in the Vocabulary Habits*). Stop writing out the new words and learning the new words anonymously. You need to be absolutely conscious of what you are building your language with. Pay attention to your use of that vocabulary in the native language.

Part 2 - Vocabulary Processing

Process some interesting words through the Vocabulary Grid *(See. Remedy 5, p. 205)*, that is through different parts of speech. This practice will increase your vocabulary stock immensely, and it will better your speaking/ writing skills considerably, too.

Part 3 - Conceptual Information

Write down the title of the book, the information about the author **and the concepts that you retrieve, reading a book.** *E g. Be the sun of your own solar system!* Write them down in a generalized form in a suggestive manner, like the impersonal messages that the author of the book sends to every one who happens to take his / her book in their hands. These concepts may be written down as pieces of advice *(We should...)*, or as the Imperative mood sentences, calling upon us to act on our imperfect nature. *(Be more self-sufficient! Rely on yourself1)*

Part 4 - The Bank of Quotes

Every good book is a well of wisdom. It's always a good idea to write out some interesting thoughts, quotations from he books you read. In this way, you will accumulate much wisdom and will always have it handy, should the need for some mental back- up arise. So, **enrich your thinking through insightful reading in English!**

Space for Notes:

Reading Changes your Intellectual Landscape!

Remedy 12

Focus on the Outcome

Now that you have completed another very important part of the book, that is remedying your Reading Skills, devote some minutes to reflecting on what you came to know in this part. Go over the most important remedies for your reading skills again.

Answer the question;

What did you come to know about...?

1. The importance of conscious reading (Chunks 1, 2)

2. Reading critically *(Chunk 3)*

3. Vocabulary channeled reading *(Remedies 1, 2)*

4. Conceptual structure of a text *(Remedy 5)*

5. The conceptually- loaded vocabulary *(Remedies 4, 5)*

6. Composition of a story *(Remedies 5, 6)*

7. Interpretation techniques *(Remedies 6, 7)*

8. The post- reading steps *(Remedy 8)*

Finally, reading is digitized nowadays and, according to Ray Kurzweil "the understanding of natural language, especially as an extension of automatic speech recognition has now entered the mainstream of science." Electronic books can hardly be deeply interpreted by readers nowadays, but I urge you to continue reading critically and let you mind develop its depth.

"Humans already constitute spiritual machines. Moreover, we will merge with the tools we are creating so closely that the distinction between human and machine will blur until the difference disappears. This process is already under way" *Ray Kurzweil*

Amazing, isn't it? But until then, let's continue reading in the fashion that we suggest above to get a lot food for thought. There are many very good academic books on the art of insightful reading. What we offer here is just a remedy to put your thinking on that track as a second language reader. The book "How to Create a Mind" by Ray Kurzweil will be very helpful.

Space for Notes:

Create an English thinking Mind!

Remedy 13

Psychological Corner
(Building up Personal Stamina)

Ending up the work on your Reading Skills, you need to rekindle the entire system of language acquisition in order **to maximize the effectiveness of language learning holistically** and boost your personal stamina that drives this learning and helps you manage your English better.

Below, we give you a mind-set formula that will boost you success in language learning, and, actually, in everything in life. Keep saying to yourself the following mental program for success. Boost your confidence and reinforce your every goal-setting with the following formula. Most importantly, believe in what you say to yourself. **Work on managing yourself to be in charge of the right language behavior better.**

"I am a strong, confident, and consistent master of my firm will.

I can...

I want to...

I will...!

I am becoming better and better in ... with each day!

Remember, at the center of the system of language learning is the **self-image**. So, back it up with the booster:

I can read in English better!

I want to read insightfully in English!

I can read consciously and enrich my English considerably!

**I am becoming more and more language-mindful
thanks to my reading in English.**

The same mental program is backing you up, both emotionally and psychologically, in your work at the pronunciation, in figuring out the grammatical structures of English, or in the expansion of your vocabulary that is forming up your thinking in English. You can apply it to practically to anything. Just keep saying to yourself these magic words:

Space for Notes:

I can..., I want to... I will...!

Remedy 14

Language Speech Profile # 6

With the completion of this part of the book, we want you to walk out of your past reading history with a sense of accomplishment. It is fundamental to your understanding of your **self-concept in English.** You have a better idea of the road map that you will continue following to the quality English. It is a controlled, action-filled, rational step in your English life. You are much more conscious of what you are rising to in the language. **Establish a constant control over your English.** Record yourself in a self-suggestive manner.

Self-Assessment

1. I have a better idea now of the main trouble spots in my perception of reading in English.

*2. I you have managed **to reason out the ways to conscious reading**.*

3. I am more conscious of the parts of speech while reading and I feel very good when I can single out the conceptually- loaded vocabulary while reading. I do not let my language slide to the automatic, mindless reading.

*4. I know how **to structure my reading conceptually** and what it means to focus on the authors messages while reading. **Reading skills upgrade my language awareness a lot!***

Now, do the rating of your Language Habits and Speech Skills **on the scale of 1 to 10**

Language Habits

1. Pronunciation Habits -

2. Grammatical Habits -

3. Vocabulary Habits -

Speech Skills

1. Listening Skills -

2. Speaking Skills -

3. Reading Skills -

4. Writing Skills -

Space for Notes:

A Correct Input Results into the Correct Output!

End of Part 4 / "Remedy Your Reading Skills"

English is Ruling the World!

You are Ruling Your English!

Remedy

Your

Listening Skills

"It's not what you tell your listeners that counts, It's what they hear".

Red Auerbach

English is Ruling the World!

You are Ruling Your English!

Section 1

The Art
Of
Listening

Information for Consideration

Establish a Mind-to-Mind Contact with a Conversation Partner!

Chunk 1

Intention and Perception

To begin with, we hope you have stopped believing by now that somehow the language will turn out to be better without your conscious effort to do so. Normally, students that think so hit the plateau, lower their expectations, and settle for less. Self-defeating behaviors, disappointment, loss of confidence that they will ever perform well, even if they tied their best, characterizes such un-achievers. But this book is not for underachievers, its for real achievers, and the people who respect the language in themselves and themselves in the language, who monitor the language evolution in themselves at every stage of learning. Listening is the micro and macro cosmos of the language, and the process of the listening skills development is also going though its **Micro, Meta, Mezzo, Macro and Super stages.** *(See Part One, Goal 8)*

We are now at the last stage of our remedying work, but **it is the stage with which any language learning actually starts.** Listening naturally grows into speech when language is accumulated by kids *(See the beginning of the book, Part Two,"The Spiral of Growth in a Second Language, p. 52).* Language action starts with listening for the kids, but it **is the final stage of language mastery for grown ups.**

Let's face it, you understand the language, but do you perceive it on the level the native language learners do? Can you grasp every word on the radio, TV, in the movies? Don't you perceive it better when you watch the body language? Do you really perceive it on both levels adequately-**the form and the content of what you hear?** I am sure that if you are honest to yourself, you will have to admit that listening, as well as the emotionally adequate use of the language, remains to be mastered much more. Try to build bridges of understanding through correct perception of your conversation partner.

Perception is a central problem in listening. *"Perception is More Important than Intent!"* The thing is, we often perceive the said word wrongly because the information was not worded out perfectly, to begin with. That is why the psycholinguistic rule" Perception is more important than intent" is so important, especially in a second / foreign language learning. **Your understanding of what was said to you depends totally**

on how clearly it was stated. Therefore, we often ask people to repeat what they said or to reword it. They normally do it, anyway, in a natural response to be perceived better. By and large, listening carefully to what is said to you directly, over any digital device, TV, the radio, etc. **requires your full aware attention.**

You need to learn to listen and to hear what is said correctly and totally, **paying attention to what is said first and how it is said next.** The best intention to communicate a thought might be lost on a listener, if this thought is not properly structured grammatically and cloaked lexically. Listening is the top skill in the constructive knowledge of a second language!.

Space for Notes:

Don't Listen without Hearing!

Chunk 2

Listen with Aware Attention!

Some one said, "Listening is being able to be changed by another person". Aware attention opens the lines of communication. You need to stay on the same wave length, establish a mind-to mind contact with the conversation partner. As a matter of fact, **the art of socializing starts with a good ability to listen and to hear.** Be present as the watcher of your mind, of your thought, of your speech, of your emotions, and of your perception of the information that enters in the form of an input into your brain. Sort this in-put out consciously!

To hit this goal, however, you need **to stop speaking or listening in the somnambulistic state** of a mind that works on the automatic pilot, unconsciously.

Do not listen with pseudo attention! Stay mentally connected to your partner! Do not clog your mind with empty stuff! Sort out the information you listen to.

Now that you are linguistically more mature, you need to listen with aware attention that helps you perceive the tenses, the passive voice, the attitude, expressed by a modal verb, the real / unreal conditioning of speech, its phrasal variety, etc, you need to consciously **pay attention to the information that is not yet in your operative use or is beyond your perception.**

Establish a mind-to mind contact with **any** speaker. Without it, you are lost, and there is no adequate communication between you and the person that is talking to you.

A Mind-to Mind Contact is a Must!

You need to **listen with aware attention** also because this is the only way to keep the conversation going. This is why you absolutely need to **develop your Responsive Skills** in English. *(See the book "Americanize Your Language, Emotionalize Your Speech)* Proper responses and conversational back-ups are indispensible in communication, and your aware attention to the points your conversation partner is making helps you use the appropriate ones.

Listening with aware attention will also help you **enrich your vocabulary considerably** because you will pay attention not only to the new words that you conversation partner might be using, but also to the part of speech that that a word belongs to. **Such listening contributes immeasurably to your correct language behavior.**

So, listen with aware attention to enhance your self confidence in the language and your growing self-esteem. Feel good with the language rooting correctly in you. **Listen consciously!**

Space for Notes:

Overcome the Inertia of Empty Listening!

English is Ruling the World!

You are Ruling Your English!

Section 2

The Choreography Of Listening

Listening Techniques

Listen to Learn and Learn to Listen!

Remedy 1

Reflect on Your Listening

We have quoted Mark Twain once above, but it's worth repeating his most meaningful words:, "The difference between the right word and almost right word is the same as between a light bug and the lightning" **Undoubtedly, only the right word imparts the right thought.**

As important as this wonderful phrase is for writers who need to be very attentive to the words that they chose to communicate their thoughts in, these beautiful words by Mark Twain are also priceless for you as a listener in aural communication.

A second language speaker needs to **discriminate between the parts of speech** while listening to his / her partners to be able to adequately understand them! **Linguistically discriminative Listening** is also aware listening when the listener pays attention to the words that he hears consciously and discriminates the parts of speech that these words belong to. Here are a few tips to follow:

1. Try to make your listening insightful and meaningful. We advise that you listen to the radio, TV; any digital device with aware attention. **The key is conscious understanding on both levels - the form and the content of the incoming information.**

2. Turn your brain radars to separate words you hear. Do not rely on the general meaning of the information you hear. **Understanding of separate words marks a growing mastery of the language of your goal.** Imagine listening to the Chinese language that you do not know. The language sounds like one inseparable and unfamiliar piece of music. But once you start learning Chinese, you begin separating the recognized words from the stream of the language. Then the number of familiar words starts growing, and initial chaos builds up into understandable small unit's first and full utterances later. The same goes about listening in English. **Momentum builds if you pay attention to that process consciously!**

3. No doubt, it is always good and helpful to listen to your partner with aware attention, especially if you **watch the body language** that helps you to put meaning together.

4. Perceive the intonation that colors anyone's speaking. The use of correct intonation always marks a native speaker from a foreigner. As a matter of fact, intonation is the top characteristics for language mastery. It, actually, explains why we prefer to speak in the native language in extremely emotional situation; arguing, fighting, etc. **Manage your intonation consciously!**

5. Don't feel ashamed to confess or admit that English is a foreign / second language to you. Ask your conversation partner to courteously repeat his / her statement. It's much better to do that than feel lost in a conversation and pretend that you follow it

Space for Notes:

Rationalize your Listening!

Remedy 2

Listen and Conceptualize

Establishing a mind-to mind contact with a speaker is essential for you to get the point that your speaker is making adequately across or to understand your conversation partner conceptually. **So, zero in on the conceptual perception of the information you listen to.** Such listening is defining native speakers, rather than foreign language users. That is why you hear English language speakers often ask you the questions like:

"What's your point?" / What's the bottom line?

We live at the most compressed time in history, and, literally, time is money for every one. A famous literary character of the two Great Russian writers Ilf and Petrov, an infamous Ostap Bender, used to say, "The time that we have is the money that we don't have." True, we are all pressed for time, so there is an urgent necessity to **economize every one's time by listening intently** for the main messages. So, the basic **tips for conceptual listening** come down to the following ones:

1. Establish a mind-to mind contact with your speaker or speakers. Listen to who talks or who the speakers are. Adjust your listening antennas to a person or people, talking to you.

2. Try to get the initial point that a speaker is making.

3. List in your mind the main concepts that a speaker is communicating to you. Details impede listening.

4. Respond while listening to back up the conversation, to expand on the speaker's point or to make inferences. Develop your Responsive skills. (See the book "Americanize Your Language, Emotionalize your Speech"). Back him / her up with sincere appreciation for any in-put.

5. Note what the bottom line of the conversation is and see if your opinion on it is asked for.

6. Be very courteous, patient, and respectful of the other person's opinion. Hear every conversation partner out.

7. Benefit from listening to some one, especially the native language speakers. Pay conscious attention to the richness of their vocabulary, the pronunciation, and the intonation of their speech, the mental picture that they create with their language in your mind.

Space for Notes:

Recharge your Social Batteries!

Remedy 3

Listen and Visualize

Throughout the book, we have been promoting the idea that **mental training has the power to change the physical structure of the brain.** We have also noted several times the significance of visualization in language learning. **Visualization is crucial in listening, too,** especially when you start discriminating different words in the stream of speech.

To better discriminate the English sounds, words, sentences, text at listening, **try to visualize the spelling of the words you hear.** You might get the meaning thanks to the context in which the unknown word was used, but **your retention of it in the memory will be ten times better if you focus on its spelling,** ask for it, or write the word down to be able to visualize it when you come across the same word again.

So, practicing visual listening, we process visual cues along with sound, physical cues and form a more conscious plane for perception. Here are some tips"

1. Obviously, visual listening is possible only with your aware attention to your partner's speaking. **Try to stay on the same wave length!** Do not think about what you are going to say in response, focus entirely on the message sent to you and visualize those parts of it that escape your understanding. Every word means something. New words that are added to your language thanks to **your aware listening modify new knowledge.**

2. Be attuned to your conversation partner emotionally and socially, too. Start you conversation with **a Small Talk**. *(See the book" Americanize Your language, Emotionalize Your Speech")* The language of conversation is primarily a language of rapport, the language of establishing connections and negotiating relationships. To avoid misinterpretations, do not feel ashamed to ask what this or that word means and writes it down immediately into your "Impeccable English" notebook, a small block note, or just a collection of index cards that serve the same purpose. Visualize the new words to get them stored better in your brain.

3. Point Your Brain Antenna to Your Conversation Partner! Failure in speaking can be traced to poor listening. Science calls listeners like that- **marginal listeners,** the listeners that do not get the feelings, only the content, or visa versa. Nudge yourself to listening better! Do not listen with pseudo attention

4. Change your social climate with some more helpful tips:

a) Avoid staying invisible in a conversation. Don't be personal or nosy.

b) Avoid using people's nicknames, or being too familiar, cavalier or negligent in listening.

c) Do not interrupt anyone, without excusing yourself.

d) Do not cut a speaker short with a negative statement.

e) Do not put anybody into a terrible spot in a conversation with a thoughtless comment.

Practice Visual Listening;
Visualize what you Hear!

Remedy 4

Manage the Sound-Alike Words

This remedy is designed for those who have difficulty with catching the meaning of some words that **sound alike, but have a different grammatical and lexical meaning**. These words are called **homonyms,** and they are often confusing for English speakers.

To tell one from another in a stream of speech, you need to focus on the place the word takes in a sentence. For example, if a confusing word is used before a noun, it's definitely an adjective., or if it has a second position in a sentence, it's most likely a verb.

So, the direct word-order in English helps us discriminate the parts of speech in listening, too. Here are some homonyms for your consideration:

1. Accept *(verb)*
E.g. We **accept** only cash.

1. Except (prep.)
*E.g. Everyone **except** Bob was present.*

2. Been *(Past Participle)*
E.g. I've **been** to that restaurant.

2. Being (Present Participle)
*You are **being** rude to me.*

3. Affect (verb)
E.g. It **affected** my decision.

3. Effect (noun)
*E.g. What was **the effect** of your decision?*

4. It's *(It is)*
E.g. **It's** my car.

4. Its (pronoun)
*E.g. The dog is in **its** place*

5. Their (Pronoun) / **There** *(adverb)*
E g. **Their** children are over there.

5. They are (subject + verb)
*E.g. **They** are my children.*

6. Weather *(noun)*
E.g. how's the **weather** today?

6. Whether (conjunction)
*E.g. I don't know **whether** he is right.*

7. Where *(adverb)* / **were** *(verb)*
E.g. **Where** were you yesterday?

7. We're *(subject + verb)*
E.g. **We're** going home.

8. Past *(noun / adjective.)*

E.g. Forget your **past**.
It's **past** life.

8. Passed *(Simple Past of the verb to pass)*
E.g. She **passed** by me a minute ago.

Space for Notes:

Expand Your Attention Span!

Remedy 5

Must Haves

We have finally come to the end of our remedial work on the language habits and speech **skills.** Remedying your Listening Skills is a very important part of your work, if not the most important one because language acquisition starts with listening. We are completing our remedial work with this part,too.

It's an adequate understanding of the language that indicates the level of your mastery in English. Also, we have indicated above that managing any skill, as well as listening skills, is a gradual process that is **going in dimensions, from the Mini dimension to the Super one,** when you understand the language like a native born.

You have been accumulating grains of knowledge from this book all along. We hope you have done that with the help of the notebook **"Impeccable English",** or you might have been recording helpful language remedy tips on the index cards with the same title.

Whatever way is more convenient for you, do it religiously. Registering the bits of knowledge that you pick here is critical for your operative memory which needs a constant back up and that helps you "grow language branches" on the "Tree of Knowledge "of English. Remember, learning a foreign language is, in fact, a life long commitment. **If you do not use it, you lose it!**

We recommend that you have your notebook" My Right Language Behavior," a set of cards, or a couple of them next to your TV set, in your car, in your purse. Be sure to jot down the words, the phrases, the bits of conversations, the responses **that engage your aware attention,** Sort them out then and there. You will be surprised how quickly you will be enriching your English and how much more language perceptive you will become.

Finally and most importantly, **get into the habit of recording yourself on a portable recorder or a cell phone**. Start with re-recording a phone message, See to it that you sound absolutely correctly and pleasantly to perceive. Listen to your voice. Assess your pronunciation, the intonation and, grammar of your speaking. Do it as often as you can until you absolutely like the way you sound in English. Be self-critical all the way!

Recording yourself is the best practice in trying to remedy a lot of imperfections in your English. It's like seeing yourself in the language and the language in you. (*See the Introduction*) As a matter of fact, this practice will do wonders to your English in time and space.

Space for Notes:

Manage Your English in Time and Space!

Remedy 6

Focus on the Outcome

Let's go over the bits of information from the section "Remedy Your Listening Skills" Refresh your memory, answering the questions below.

Reflect on your perception of the tips on your Listening Skills.

1. What does conscious listening mean? (Chunk 1)

2. What is the implication of the psycholinguistic statement "Perception is more important than intent"? (Chunk 1)

3. What does listening with aware attention entail? Why do we call it "aware attention"? (Chunk 2)

4. Why is it important to reflect on your listening abilities in English? (Remedy1)

5. What makes your listening in English insightful? (Remedy 1)

6. What does the practice of conceptualizing information that you hear mean? Why is it crucial for business? (Remedy 2)

7. Visualization is a great tool of our brain, right? How does it help you in your listening? (Remedy 3)

8. What are homonyms? Does being aware of them help understand English better? (Remedy 4)

9. How does proficiency in the listening skills add to the total language performance in English?

Language is One Unified Whole!

10. Finally, give yourself the final boost for remedying your English psychologically, mentally, emotionally and physically. You've done a great job, propelling your English and yourself in this life!

Space for Notes:

Language Competence + Speech Performance = Language Consciousness!

Remedy 7

Language - Speech Profile # 7

With the completion of this part of the book, you walk out of your past Second Language history with a new sense of accomplishment. It is fundamental to your understanding of your **self-concept in English.** You have a better idea of the road map that you will continue following to the quality English. You have learnt to listen, speak, read, and write with a conscious control over your English. Do the final reflection work on your English. **Record the Ultimate Result of your remedying the langu**age.

Self-Assessment

1. I have a better idea now of the main trouble spots in my listening skills.

2. I have managed to reason out the ways of bettering every skill in English.

3. I am more conscious of the language peculiarities while listening, speaking, reading and writing in English, and I feel very good when I perceive English correctly both grammatically and lexically. I do not let my language slide to the automatic listening, speaking, reading, or writing with many uncorrected mistakes that pollute my English any more.

4. I continue to grow the language in me through conscious listening, speaking, listening and writing. Conscious does it!

In view of the changes in your speech skills, do **the final holistic rating of your Language Habits and Speech Skills** on the scale of **1 to 10.**

Language Habits

1. Pronunciation Habits -

2. Grammatical Habits -

3. Vocabulary Habits -

Speech Skills

1. Listening Skills -

2. Speaking Skills -

3. Reading Skills -

4. Writing Skills -

Space for Notes:

Control your English, or English will Control you!

Remedy 8

The Ultimate Picture of You!
(Building up Personal Stamina)

Ending our tough remedial work at your language habits and speech skills, we need **to maximize the effectiveness of your linguistic apprenticeship.** It was an exciting endeavour on your part Now, boost your personal stamina for the last time, but in a little different way

Every one of us is in need of psychological support- **the support of self-respect.** Every one of us gets criticized by our parents, friends, colleagues, husbands, wives, bosses, by the people we love most. We get criticized even by neighbors and passers-by. There is only one person who always supports us or backs us up in any undertaking, the only one who understands us like no one else, the only one who feels our pain when we cry and the joy when we smile. **This person is you!**

You can apply self-support to practically anything **to change the ultimate picture of anything that you choose to do.** Your self-support gives your psyche a boost and your brain an emotional up-lift. You helped yourself emotionally to master a foreign language. Emotional intelligence is needed to do that.

The Method of the Conscious Language Behavior is actually, building the new living intelligence in you, and you have managed to be consistent in doing it. It is so tantalizing to think about **the vastness of the concept of intelligen**ce and the place of your own language intelligence in it that, I am sure, you would very much like to monitor it knowingly.

By living intelligence, we mean the state of deep consciousness and mental clarity in the language. You have stepped out of your relative, mechanical, emotional hullabaloo knowledge of English and started enjoying **the conscious, operative, and optimal state of your language / speech competence.** You know now that only conscious mind is responsible for the adequate verbal expression! Only conscious mind removes the self-inhibitions and helps you establish the self-evaluation of the rightness or wrongness of the language actions you are about to implement. Very soon, you will have an inspiring sensation of a new feeling in the language thanks to your right language behavior.

Most importantly, keep working out at your **self-respect philosophy; plant new seeds** of success into your mind each day. Your brain gets the confidence vibrations and transmits them to your mind that starts helping you formulate your thoughts in English.

The noted neuroscientist Michael Mezmenich has shown that **our brains can adapt to change if we really focus on the change. He showed that "the shape of your brain maps changes** depending upon what we do over the course of our lives". *("Mystery of Science" by Michael Mezmenich)*

Obviously, the mind is in charge of your English! It has become much more correct in grammar, richer in vocabulary, more structured in writing, and much more flexible in communication. Keep helping it to stay in good shape with the help of the psychological boosters and emotional uplifts. That is the psycholinguistic approach that we are practicing here.

And always remembers the rule at the bottom of this page. **Be the Star of Your Life!** But mind you, though, that it is impossible to accomplish this goal unless you radiate kindness and generosity and **create the space of synergy** around you **socially, culturally, professionally and physically** with the help of the right language behavior.

Kindness and Generosity

Make kindness and generosity

Your life's velocity!

Kindness creates the space

In which you are welcome face-to-face

Generosity surprises you

And makes you change your point of view

Both qualities enrich

Your personal outreach

And make you a better fan

Of a longer life span!

Space for Notes:

Be the Star of Your Life!

End of Book Three" Remedy Your Speech Skills"

Book Four

Speech Odyssey / Impeccable English

Impeccable English

Train Your Language / Speech Musculature!

English is Ruling the World!

You are Ruling Your English!

Section 1

Trouble Shooting

Put your Language in Rapport with Speech!

Trouble Spot 1

Tips on the Questions at hand

We are not presenting here the cases of wrong, uncontrolled English for you to correct. By now, you have, most certainly, realized what trouble spots you need to fix. We find it to be much more beneficial for you **to fortify the correct speech skills,** for them not to slide back to hullabaloo English Below; you will find the tips on the questions at hand, presented in 5 main tenses. Even though it might seem to be a piece of cake for you to ask these questions, do not skip this part. Rather, **take a piece of paper, close the right side of the list** where the **Yes/ No and Wh. Questions** are written and see how well you can ask / write them yourself. This work can be identified as the left - right brain hemispheres at work. The left side is responsible for the form of the language, the right one for its content. Play them out! **Conscious makes it certain!** This work is the same as **the warming up exercises** for a pianist who does simple note playing before he demonstrates his excellence at playing a symphony. **Record this self-interviewing.** Like the way you sound in English.

IDENTITY INFORMATION

The Simple Present Tense, Two Types of Questions (the verb "to be")

1	**First Name** My name is John. - I see, thank you. ⟵	1. Is your first naming John? -Yes, it is. / No, it's not. 2. **What's your first name**, please? -It is John.
2	**Last Name** My last name is Gonzales.	1. Is your last name Ray? No, it isn't. / No, it's not. 2. **What's your last name**, please? It is Gonzales

---

3	**Age**
	
	I am 24 years old.
		1. Are you 21 years old?
		   -Yes, I am. / No, I'm not.
		2. **How old are you?**
		   I'm 24.(years old)

4	**Nationality**
	
	I am Colombian.
		1. Are you Peruvian??
		   - No, I'm not.
		2. **What's your nationality?**
		   I'm Colombian.

5	**Country**
	
	I am from Colombia.
		1. Are you from Brazil/?
		   - No, I'm not.
		2. **What country are you from?**
		   -I'm from Colombia.

6	**City**
	
	I am from New York.
	-
		1. Are you from Stamford?
		   - No, I'm not.
		2. **What city are you from?**
		   -I'm from New York.

7	**Address**
	
	My address is 32 Beach St.
		1. Is your address 36 Beech St.?
		   - No, it isn't.
		2. **What's your address,** please?
		   -It is 32 Beech St.

8	**Telephone Number**
	
	My phone number is
	531-650.
		1. Is your telephone number
		   531-6508?
		   -Yes, it is. / No, it isn't.
		2. **What's your phone number,**
		   please?
		   -It is 531-6508

9	**Marital Status**
	
	I am single.
		1. Are you married?
		   -Yes, I'm. / (No I'm not.)
		2. **What's your marital status,**
		   please?
		   -I am single

10	**Citizenship** I am a US citizen.	1. Are you a US citizen? -Yes, I am. / No, I'm not. 2. **What's your citizenship,** please? I am an American citizen.
11	**Legal Status** I am a permanent resident. I have a green card.	1. Are you a permanent resident? Yes, I am. / No, I'm not. 2. **What's your legal status**, please? I am a permanent USA resident
12	**Job** I am a computer engineer at Apples.	1. Are you a computer designer? -Yes, I am. / No, I'm not 2. **What's your job**, please It is a computer engineer at Apples.
13	**Education** I have a BA in Computer Science.	1. Do you have a bachelor's degree? -Yes, I do./ No. I don't. 2. **What's your education**, please? - I have a BA in Computer science.

SIMPLE ENGLISH AT HAND

Yes / No and Wh. questions

Main Grammar Structures		**The Simple Present Tense** Focus on the verb **"to be"**
1	**It is...** It is a car	1. Is it a car? - Yes, it is. / No, it isn't. 2. **What is it?** - It's a car
2	**This is...** This is a book	1. Is this a book? Yes, it is. / No, it isn't. 2. **What's this?** This is a book

3	**That is...**
	
	That is a house over there.
		1. Is that a house over there?
		   - Yes, it is. / No, it isn't.
		2. **What's that**?
		   - That is a house

4	**They are...**
	
	They are students.
		1. Are they students?
		   - Yes, they are. / No, they aren't.
		2. **What are they**?
		   - They are students.

5	**These are...**
	
	These are books.
		1. Are these books?
		   Yes, they are. / No, they are not.
		2. **What are these**?
		   - These are books

6	**He is...**
	
	He is a student.
		1. Is he a student?
		   -Yes, he is. / No, he isn't.
		2. **What is he?**
		   - He is a student

7	**She is...**
	
	She is a doctor.
		1. Is she a nurse?
		   - Yes, she is. / No, she isn't
		2. **What is she?**
		   - She is a doctor

8	**They are...**
	
	They are truck drivers.
		1. Are they students?
		   - No, they are not
		2. **What is their profession**?
		   - They are truck drivers.

9	**Possession**
	
	It is my book.
		1. Is it your book?
		   -Yes, it is. / No, it isn't.
		2. **Whose book is it?**
		   - It is my book

10	**Kind** It is a good car.	1. Is it a good car? -Yes, it is. / No, it isn't. 2. **What kind of car is it?** - It is a good car
11	**Color** It's a red car.	1. Is it a red car? -Yes, it is. / No, It isn't. 2. **What color is it?** - It is a red car / It's red.
12	**Place (Location)** The car is on the street	1. Is the car on the street? Yes, it is. / No, it isn't. 2. **Where is the car?** - The car is on the street
13	**Objects + Place** **There** is a book **on the table.** **There are** two cars **in the street.**	1. Is there a book on the table? -Yes, there is. / No, there isn't. **What is there in the street?** 2. **How many cars are there** in the street? - There are two cars on the street
14	**Uncountable (+ some, any, no)** There is **some** water in the cup. Is there **any** water in the cup? There is **no** water in the cup.	1. **Is** there **any** water in the cup? - Yes, there is. / No, there isn't. 2. **How much water is there in the cup?** - There is some water in the cup
15	**Price** It is 5 dollars.	1. **Is it 5 dollars?** - Yes, it is. / No, it isn't. 2. **How much is it?** - It is 5 dollars

16	Cost The dress costs 25 dollars.	1. **Does** the dress **cost** 25 dollars/ - Yes, it does. / No, it doesn't. 2. **How much does it cost?** - It **costs** 25 dollars.
17	**State** I am - sick /terrific /great - OK./awesome /fine - lonesome. / a little down - happy./ excited	1. Are you OK? - Yes, I am. / No, I'm not 2. **How are you?** - I am absolutely terrific!
18	**Impersonal English** It is important to be computer- literate these days.	1. Is it important to be computer-literate these days? - Absolutely. 2. **What is important these days?** - It is important to be computer- literate.
19	**Assessment** It is a good job. -	1. Is it a good job? -Yes, it is. / No, isn't. 2. **What do you make of** that **job?** -It is a great job.

20. *It's important*
necessary
interesting
easy } *for me* { *to learn English.*
hard
expensive

to learn English.
to pay the bills
to watch this movie.
to operate a computer.
to find a job.
to buy a brand new car.

21. *Is it important for you to send that email to him?* - *It sure is.*

22. *Is it hard to find a job in new York?* - *Pretty much so.*

23. *Is it expensive to buy a bike?* - *Not really. It's pretty affordable.*

THE SIMPLE PRESENT TENSE

Questions with the verb "to have" in different word-combinations

1	**Possession** (to have something) I have a car./ a house /a bike	1. Do you have a car?/ Have you got a car? -Yes, I do. / No, I don't./ Yes, I have. 2. **What do you have? / What have you got?** -I have a car / I've got a car.
2	**Possession** (3d person sg.) He has a beautiful house	1. Does he have a beautiful house? -Yes, he does. / No, he doesn't. 2. **What kind of house does he have?** -He has a beautiful house.
3	**To have breakfast** I have breakfast at 8 o'clock	1. Do you have breakfast at 8 o'clock? -Yes, I do. No, I don't. 2. **At what time do you have breakfast?** -I have a breakfast at 8 o'clock.
4	**To have lunch** I have lunch at 1 o'clock	1. Do you have lunch at 1 o'clock? -Yes, I do. / No, I don't. 2. **Who has lunch at 1 o'clock?** -I do
5	**To have a break** I have a break at 12 o'clock.	1. Do you have a break at 12 o'clock? -Yes, I do. / No, I don't. 2. **What time do you have a break?** -I have a break at 1 o'clock.
6	**Family** I have a family here.	1. Do you have a family here? / **Have you got..?** -Yes, I do. / No, I don't. / Yes, I have. 2. **Who has a family here?/** - I do /

7	To have a Job I have a job.	1. Do you have a job? / Have you got a job? -Yes, I do. / No, I don't. / Yes, I have. 2. **What job do you have?/ have you got?** - I am a carpenter./ I've got a good job.
8	To have an appointment I have a job appointment	1. Do you have an appointment? -Yes, I do. / No, I don't. 2. **When do you have an appointment?** - I have it at 2 p.m. today.
9	To have an interview I have an interview on Monday.	1. Do you have an interview on Monday? -Yes I do. / No, I don't. 2. **When do you have an interview?** - I have it on Monday.
10	To have a problem I have a problem with my computer.	1. Do you have a problem with your computer? -Yes, I do. (No, I don't) 2. **What problem do you have?** - I have a problem with the Internet. **What's wrong?** - Something is wrong with the Internet.
11	To have an opportunity I have an opportunity to be admitted to college.	1. Do you have an opportunity to…? -Yes, I do.. / No, I don't. 2. **What opportunity do you have?** -I have an opportunity to be admitted to college.

12	**To have money** I have some money.	1. Do you have any money on you? -Yes, I do / No, I don't. 2. **How much money do you have on you?** - I have a couple of dollars.
13	*To have time* *I have some time now* **To have +a noun** *To have an appointment* *To have (no) money* *To have a vocation* --	1. *Do you have time right now?* *-Yes, I actually do. / Sorry, I don't.* 2. *How much time do you have?* *-I have half an hour to do that job* *- I've got an hour.* ***I have / I've got a job appointment*** ***He has no money to buy a car.*** ***We have a vocation in June.***

THE SIMPLE PAST TENSE

Two Questions with the verb "to do" in different word-combinations

1	**To do morning exercises** I did my morning exercise yesterday	1. Did you do morning exercise yesterday? Yes I did. (No, I didn't) 2. **When did you do morning exercise?** - I did them yesterday.
2	**To do shopping** I did my food shopping	1. Did you do your food shopping? Yes I did. (No, I didn't) 2. **What did you do?** I did my food shopping

3	**To do cooking**
	
	I did some cooking yesterday
		1. Did you do any cooking yesterday?
		   Yes I did. (No, I didn't)
		2. **When did I do some cooking?**
		   I did it yesterday

4	**To do the laundry**
	I did my laundry last week
		1. Did you do your laundry last week?
		   Yes, I did. (No, I didn't)
		2. **Who did his laundry last week?**
		   I did.

5	**To do the bills**
	I did my bills on Saturday
		1. Did you do your bills on Saturday?
		   Yes, I did. (No, I didn't)
		2. **What did you do on Saturday?**
		   I did my bills on Saturday

6	**To do the paper work**
	I did my paper work last week.
		1. Did you do your paper work last week?
		   Yes, I did. (No, I didn't)
		2. **When did you do your paper work?**
		   I did it last week.

7	**To do some ironing**
	I did my ironing on Friday
		1. Did I do your ironing on Friday?
		   Yes, I did. (No, I didn't)
		2. **When did you do your ironing?**
		   I did it on Friday

8	**To do the research**
	I did some research on the computer.
		1. Did I do any research on the computer?
		   Yes, I did. (No, I didn't)
		2. **Who did some research on the computer?**
		   I did.

9	**To do the homework** I did my homework on time.	1. Did you do your homework on time? Yes, I did. (No, I didn't) 2. **Who did his homework?** I did
10	**To do some vacuuming** I did some vacuuming at home.	1. Did you do your vacuuming? Yes, I did. (No, I didn't) 2. **Where did you do some vacuuming?** I did it at home.
11	**To do some gardening** She did some gardening last weekend.	1. Did she do any gardening? Yes, she did. (No, she didn't) 2. **What did she do?** She did some gardening
12	**To do some planning** I did some planning for a weekend.	1. Did you do your planning yesterday? Yes, I did. (No, I didn't) 2. **When did you do your planning?** I did it yesterday
13	**To do the hair** I did my hair in the morning	1. Did you do the hair in the morning? Yes, I did. (No, I didn't) 2. **When did you do your hair?** I did it in the morning
14	**To do the nails** She did her nails yesterday	1. Did she do her nails yesterday? Yes, I did. (No, I didn't) 2. **Who did her nails yesterday?** She did.

15	**To have the nails done** I had my nails done last week.	1. Did you have your nails done last week? Yes, I did. (No, I didn't) 2. **When did you have your nails done?** I had them done last week.
16	**To have the hair done** I had my hair done yesterday	1. Did you have your hair done yesterday? Yes, I did. (No, I didn't) 2. **When did you have your hair done?** I had it done yesterday
17	**To have work done** She had her work done by them.	1. Did she have her work done? Yes, she did. (No, she didn't) 2. What did she have done by them? She had her work done
18	**To have the car fixed.** I had my car fixed last week.	1. Did you have your car fixed? Yes, I did. (No, I didn't) 2. **When did you have your car fixed?** I had it fixed last week.

THE SIMPLE PAST TENSE
Yes / No questions + Wh. Questions

(Word-combinations with t commonly used verbs)

1	**To get up** I got up at 7 yesterday	1. Did you get up at 7 a.m. yesterday - Yes, I did. (No I didn't) 2. **What time did you get up yesterday?** - I got up at 7 a.m. yesterday

2	**To take a shower** I took a shower at 7:00 am	1. Did you take a shower at 7 am? - Yes, I did. (No, I didn't) 2. **What did you take at 7 am?** - I took a shower at 7 am
3	**To have a breakfast** I had breakfast at 7:30.	1. Did you have a breakfast at 7; 30/? - Yes, I did. (No, I didn't) 2. **At what time did you have breakfast?** - I had it at 7: 30.
4	**To get dressed** I got dressed after that	1. Did you get dressed after that? Yes, I did. (No, I didn't) 2. **When did you get dressed?** I got dressed after that
5	**It took me some time...** It took me 20 min. to get ready	1. Did it take you 20 minutes to get ready? Yes, it did. (No, it didn't) 2. **How long did it take you to get ready?** It took me 20 min to get ready
6	**To leave home** I left home at 8 am	1. Did you leave home at 8 am? Yes, I did. (No, I didn't) 2. **At what time did you leave home?** I left home at 8 am
7	**To drive to work** I drove to work	1. Did you drive to work? - Yes, I did. (No, I didn't) 2. **How did you get to work??** - I drove
8	**To work in the office** I worked in the office yesterday	1. Did you work in the office yesterday? Yes I did. (No, I didn't) 2. **Where did you work yesterday?** I worked in the office yesterday

9	**To receive people at work** I received people on Monday	1. Did you receive people on Monday? Yes I did. (No, I didn't) 2. **When did you receive people?** I received people on Monday
10	**To make phone calls** I made some calls at work	1. Did you make any phone calls at work? Yes, I did. (No, I didn't) 2. **Whom did you make some calls to?** I made them to my business associates.
11	**To talk to somebody** I talked to my friend on Skype.	1. Did I talk to your friend on Skype? Yes, I did. (No, I didn't) 2. **Whom did you talk to on Skype?** I talked to my friend
12	**To be worried about something / somebody** I was worried about my loved ones.	1. Were you worried about your loved ones? - Yes, I was. (No, I wasn't) 2. **Whom were you worried about?** - I was worried about my son
13	**To bother someone** That problem bothered me a lot	1. Did that problem bother you a lot? Yes, it did. (No, it didn't) 2. **What bothered you a lot?** That problem did.
14	**To buy a brand new car** He bought a brand new car	1. Did he buy a brand new car? Yes, he did. (No, he didn't) 2. **What kind of car did he buy?** He bought a Toyota.
15	**To eat out** We ate out on Sunday.	1. Did you eat out on Sunday? Yes, we did. (No, we didn't) 2. **When did you eat out?** We ate out on Sunday.

16	**To drink a cup of coffee.** I drank a cup of coffee in the morning.	1. Did you drink a cup of coffee? Yes, I did. (No, I didn't) 2. **What did you drink?** I drank a cup of coffee
17	**To watch TV** I watched TV in the evening.	1. Did you watch TV in the evening? Yes, I did. (No, I didn't) 2. **What did you do in the evening?** I watched TV
18	**To meet someone** I met a friend in the bar.	1. Did you meet a friend in the bar? - Yes, I did. (No, I didn't) 2. **Whom did you meet in the bar?** - I met a friend there
19	**To see the doctor** I saw the doctor yesterday	1. Did you I see the doctor yesterday? - Yes I did. (No, I didn't) 2. **When did you see the doctor?** - I saw him yesterday
20	**To tell somebody the story** I told her the story	1. Did you tell her the story? - Yes, I did. (No, I didn't) 2. **What did you tell her?** - I told her the story
21	**To see a movie** I saw a great movie	1. Did you see a great movie? - Yes I did. (No, I didn't) 2. **What kind of movie did you see?** - I saw a great movie
22	**To do the homework** I did my homework	1. Did you I do your homework? - Yes, I did. (No, I didn't) 2. **What did you do?** - I did my homework

23	**To call a friend** I called my friend	1. Did you call your friend? - Yes, I did. (No, I didn't) 2. **Who did you call?** - I called my friend
24	**To discuss something** We discussed our plans for the weekend.	1. Did you discuss your plans? - Yes, we did. (No, we didn't) 2. **What did you discuss?** - We discussed our plans for the weekend.
25	**To take a bath** I took a bath	1. Did you take a bath? Yes, I did. (No, I didn't) 2. **What did you take?** I took a bath

Mind you! The Simple Past Tense expresses a regular past action. It is used in narration. So, in telling a story, use the past tenses. Stick with the rule Past + Past, narrating anything.

THE SIMPLE FUTURE TENSE

Yes / No questions / Wh. Questions

1	**Date** It will be the 1st of April tomorrow	1. Will it be the 1st of April tomorrow? - Yes, it will. (No, it will not) 2. **What date will it be tomorrow?** - It'll be the 1st of April tomorrow
2	**Day of the week** It will be Wednesday tomorrow	1. Will it be Wednesday tomorrow? - Yes, it will. (No, it will not) 2. **What day will it be tomorrow?** - It'll be Wednesday tomorrow

3	**Time**
	 It will be at 8 o'clock
		1. Will it be at 8 o'clock
		    - Yes, it will. (No, it will not)
		 2. **What time will it be?**
		    - It'll be at 8 o'clock

4	**This**
	 This will be fine
		1. Will this be fine?
		    Yes, this will. (No, this will not)
		 2. **What will be fine?**
		    This job will.

5	**That**
	 That won't help me.
		1. Will that help you?
		    -Yes, it will. (No, that won't help me.)
		 2. **Why won't that help you?**
		    - It'll be too late, you know.

6	**Possession**
	 It will be my car soon
		1. Will it be your car soon?
		    Yes, it will. (No, it will not)
		 2. **Whose car will it be soon?**
		    It'll be mine.

7	**Kind**
	 It will be an expensive car
		1. Will it be an expensive car?
		    Yes it will. (No, it will not)
		 2. **What kind of car will it be?**
		    It will be an expensive car

8	**Color**
	 It will be white
		1. Will it be white?
		    Yes, it will. (No, it will not)
		 2. **What color will it be?**
		    It will be white

9	**Location**
	 It will take place in the Times Square.
		1. Will it take place in New York?
		    - Yes, it will. (No, it will not)
		 2. **Where will it take place?**
		    - It'll take place in the Times Square.

10	**Object and place** There will be many people there	1. Will there be many people there? - Yes, there will. (No, there won' t) 2. **How many people will there be?** - There will thousands of people there
11	**Price** It will be about $20	1. Will it about $ 20? Yes, it will. (No, it won't) 2. **How much will it be?** It will about $ 20
12	**State** She will be pleased./ upset/ excited /aggravated / happy / disappointed.	1. Will she be pleased? - Yes, she will. (No, she will not) 2. **Who will she be pleased?** - She will.
13	**Impersonal** It will be hard to do it easy/ impossible/ fun / challenging / tough.	1. Will it be hard to do it? - Yes, it sure will. (No, it won't) 2. **What will it be like?** - It will be fun.
14	**Assessment** It will be well-done./ great / impeccable / sloppy / unacceptable	1. Will it be well-done? - Yes, it will. (No, it won't) 2. **How will it be done?** - It will be great!/ That'll be great1
15	**Reason** It will be impossible to do because…	1. Will it be possible to do? - Yes, it will. (No. I don't think so.) 2. **Why will it be impossible to be done?** - It will be impossible to do it because…

16	**Work** I will have to work tomorrow	1. Will you have to work tomorrow? - Yes I will. (No, I won't) 2. **How come you'll have to work tomorrow?** - I'll have to make up for a sick day
17	**Plans** We will go to the movies.	1. Will you go to the movies? - Yes, we will. (No, we won't) 2. **Where will you go?** - We'll go to the movie
18	**O.K.** Everything will be OK	1. Will it be OK? - Sure. (No, I don't think so.) 2. **When will it be OK?** - It will be OK tomorrow
19	**A date** I will have a date on Sunday	1. Will you have a date on Sunday? - Yes, I will. (No, I won't) 2. **When will you I have a date?** - I'll have it on Sunday
20	**Departure** I will leave at 5 pm / I will be leaving	1. Will you leave at 5 pm? - Yes I will. (No, I will not) 2. **At what time will you leave?** - I will leave at 5 pm
21	**Purchase** I will buy this book later	1. Will you buy it later? - Yes. I will. (No, I will not) 2. What will you buy later? - I will buy this book later
22	**A phone call** I will give her a call tonight	1. Will you give her a call tonight? - Yes, I will. (No, I won't) 2. **Whom will you give a call tonight?** - I will give her a call tonight

23	**An apology** I will apologize to her	1. Will I apologize to her? - Yes, I will. (No, I will not) 2. **Who will I apologize to her?** I- will.
24	**News** It will be great news for me.	1. Will it be great news for you? Yes, it sure will. (No, it will not) 2. **What kind of news will it be?** It will be great news for me.
25	**Weekend** It will be a fun weekend	1. Will it be a great weekend? Yes, it will. (No, it won't) 2. **What kind of weekend will be it?** It will be a fun weekend
26	**Promise** I will give her a promise to do it on time.	1. Will you give her a promise? I sure will. (No, I don't think so.) 2. Whom will you give a promise? I'll give it to her.
27	**Dinner** I 'll have dinner with him	1. Will you have a dinner with him? - Yes, I will. (No, I won't) 2. **Whom will you have dinner with?** - I' ll have it with him
28	**Party** I' ll go to a party on Saturday	1. Will you go to a party on Saturday? - Yes, I sure will. (No, I won't) 2. **When will you go to the party?** - I 'll go to the party on Saturday
29	**Celebration** We'll celebrate my birthday this weekend	1. Will you celebrate your birthday on weekend? - Yes, we will. (No, we will not) 2. **What will we celebrate this weekend?** - We'll celebrate my birthday this weekend

THE PRESENT PROGRESSIVE TENSE

Yes or No questions /Wh. Questions

1	**Being** She is being nasty./ rude / impolite / demanding / mean	1. Is she being nasty? - Yes, she sure is. (No, she's not) 2. **Who is being nasty?** - She is.
2	**Having** They are having dinner now.	1. Are they having dinner now? - Yes, they are. (No, they aren't) 2. **What are they having?** - They're having dinner
3	**Doing** She is doing her job pretty well.	1. Is she doing her job? - Yes, she is. (No, she's not) 2. **How is she doing her job?** - She's doing it pretty well.
4	**Calling** **Mary is** calling John right now.	1. Is Mary calling John right now? - Yes, she is. (No, she's not) 2. **Whom is Mary calling**? - She's calling John
5	**Coming** She is coming	1. Is she coming? - Yes, she is. (No, she isn't) 2. **Who is coming?** - She is.
6	**Going** *(movement)* I am going home	1. Are you going home? - Yes, I am. (No, I'm not) 2. **Where are you going?** - I'm going home

7	**Going to do** s.t. *(intention)* I am going **to watch** T.V.	1. Are you going to watch T.V.? - Yes, I am. (No, I'm not) 2. **What are you going to do?** - I am going to watch T.V.
8	**Studying** She is studying English	1. Is she studying English? - Yes, she is. (No, she's not) 2. **What language is she studying/** - She's studying English
9	**Laughing** They are laughing at me	1. Are they laughing at you? - Yes, they are. (No, they aren't) 2. **Who is laughing at you?** - They are.
10	**Happening** Something is happening over there	1. Is anything happening over there? - Yes, it's. (No, it's not) 2. **What is happening over there?** - Something is.
11	**Talking** They are talking about me	1. Are they talking about me? - Yes, they are. (No, they're not) 2. **Whom are they talking about?** - They're talking about you.
12	**Buying** He is buying food	1. Is he buying food? - Yes, he is. (No, he's not) 2. **What is he buying?** - He is buying food
13	**Eating** They are eating pizza.	1. Are they eating lunch? - Yes, they are. (No, they're not) 2. **What are they eating?** - They're eating pizza.

14	**Drinking** He is drinking tea / coffee / milk /some soft drink / juice /some beverage, etc.	1. Is he drinking tea? - Yes, he is. (No, he isn't. 2. **What is he drinking?** - He is drinking tea
15	**Leaving** He is leaving tomorrow.	1. Is he leaving tomorrow? Yes, he is. (No, he's not) 2. **Who is leaving tomorrow?** He is.
16	**Wearing** She is wearing a nice blouse	1. Is she wearing a nice blouse? Yes, she is. (No, she's not) 2. **What kind of blouse is she wearing?** She is wearing a nice blouse
17	**Working** My relationship with John isn't working.	1. Is your relationship with John working? - Yes, actually is. (Not really.) 2. **Why isn't your relationship with John working?** -He's too much into himself, you know.

THE PRESENT PERFECT TENSE

Yes or No questions / Wh. Questions

1	**Accomplishment** I have finished my project this year	1. Have you finished your project this year? Yes, I have. (No, I haven't) 2. **What have you done this year?** I've finished my project this year

2	**Deposit** She has deposited her check in the bank	1. Has she deposited her check in the bank? Yes, she has. (No, she hasn't) 2. **What has she deposited in the bank?** She's deposited her check in the bank
3	**Trip** He has been on a good trip	1. Has he been on a good trip? Yes, he has. (No, he hasn't) 2. **Who has been on a good trip?** He has.
4	**Phone call** She has not called me today	1. Has she called you today? Yes, she has. (No, she hasn't) 2. **How come she hasn't called you today?** I guess, she's forgotten to do it.
5	Order I have ordered a new sink for my bathroom.	1. Have you ordered a new sink? Yes, I have. (No, I haven't) 2. **What have you ordered?** I've ordered a new sink form my bathroom.
6	**Purchase** She has bought a new dress	1. Has she bought a new dress? - Yes, she has. (No, she hasn't) 2. **What has she bought?** - She's bought a new dress
7	**Work** I have done my work / I **am done** with my work.	1. Have you done your work? - Yes, I have. (No, I haven't) 2. **What have you done?** - I've done my work

8	**Result**
	I have written a good business report.
		1. Have you written a good business report?
		  - Yes, I have. (No, I haven't)
		2. **What kind of report have you written?**
		  - I've written a good report.

9	**A good sale**
	He has made a great sale
		1. Has he made a great sale?
		  - Yes, he has. (No, he hasn't)
		2. **Who has made a great sale?**
		  - He has.

10	**Appointment**
	She has set up an appointment
		1. Has she set up an appointment?
		  - Yes, she has. (No, she hasn't)
		2. **Who has set up an appointment?**
		  - She has.

11	**Movie**
	I have seen a good movie
		1. Have I seen a good movie?
		  - Yes, I have. (No, I haven't)
		2. **Who has seen a good movie?**
		  - I have.

12	**Meals**
	I have cooked three meals today
		1. Have I cooked three meals today?
		  - Yes, I have. (No, I haven't)
		2. **Who has cooked three meals today?**
		  - I have

13	**Drink**
	They have drunk beer
		1. Have they drunk beer?
		  - Yes, the have. (No, they haven't)
		2. **What have they drunk?**
		  - They've drunk beer

14	**Departure**
	He has left for England
		1. Has he left for England?
		  Yes, he has. (No, he hasn't)
		2. **Where has he left?**
		  He's left for England

15	**Commitment** He has not made any commitment to her yet	1. Hasn't he made any commitment yet? - Yes, he has. (No he hasn't) 2. **Who hasn't made any** **commitment?** - He hasn't.
16	**Plans** I have made my plans for the weekend.	1. Have you made any plans for the weekend? - Yes, I have. (Not really.) 2. **What plans have you made?** - I've planned to go to Manhattan.
17	**Project** I have concluded my project	1. Have you concluded your project? - Yes, I have. (No, I haven't) 2. **What have you concluded?** - I've concluded my project
18	**Devotion** He has devoted the song to his wife.	1. Has he devoted the song to her wife? - Yes, he has. (No, he hasn't) 2. **Whom has he devoted the song to?** - He's devoted it to her wife
19	**A gift** He has gotten a nice gift	1. Has he gotten a nice gift? - Yes, he has. (No, he hasn't) 2. **What has he gotten?** - He's gotten a nice gift
20	**Payment** She has paid her bills this month	1. Has she paid her bills this month? - Yes, she has. (No, she hasn't) 2. What has she paid this month? - She's paid her bills.
21	**Meal** I have had a good meal	1. Have you had a good meal? - Yes, I have. (No, I haven't) 2. **What kind of meal have I had?** - I've had a really good meal

22	**e-mail** He has e-mailed me today	1. Has he e-mailed you today? -Yes, he has. (No, he hasn't) 2. **What has he done?** - He's e-mailed me today
23	**Discussion** We have not discussed that problem.	1. Have you discussed that problem? - Yes, we have. (No, we haven't) 2. **What haven't you discussed?** - We've discussed that problem.
24	**Invitation** I have invited them for dinner	1. Have you invited them for dinner? - Yes, I have. (no, I haven't) 2. **Whom have you invited for dinner?** - I've invited them for dinner
25	**Praise** She has praised me a lot	1. Has she praised me a lot? - Yes, she has. (No she hasn't) 2. **Whom has she praised a lot**? - She has praised me a lot
26	**Success** She has been a great success ever since	1. Has she been a great success ever since? - Yes, she has. (No, she hasn't) 2. Who has been a great success ever since? - She has
27	**Failure** He has failed the math exam.	1. Has he ever failed the math exam? - Yes, he has. (No, he hasn't) 2. **What has he failed in**? - He's failed the math exam.
28	**Victory** They have won the game	1. Have they won the game? - Yes, the have. (No, they haven't) 2. **What have they won**? - They've won the game

29	**Conclusion** She has concluded her speech successfully	1. Has she concluded her speech successfully? - Yes, he has. (No, she hasn't) 2. **How has she concluded her** **speech?** - She's concluded it successfully

Thanks. **You've done a great job!** But, remember, **your brain is very perceptive to persistence.** So, try to control every sentence religiously until your habit of the correct language behavior is formed. Gradually, asking and answering questions will become a piece of cake. Also, pay attention to the intonation when answering that question! The information that is asked should be accentuated more with **the falling tone of voice.** *(Check with Part Two" Pronunciation Habits')* Your English will gradually come to the point when you will need no control over your conscious mind. **Your subconscious mind will take charge of your correct behavior in English,** and your English speaking will almost as sure, confident, and correct, as your native language speaking is. Such state of your language competence will signify the formation of your **English language consciousness.** Go for it!

Use your Mind to change your Brain!

Trouble Spot 2

Ask Question to any Part of a Sentence

1. *In Part Three of the book, Remedies 5 and 7*, we are remedying your Question-Answer skills, drawing you aware attention to the idea that you can ask information any of the 4 types of questions in English to any part of the sentence. We make it easier for you, by organizing those questions according to the word- order in a sentence. In life, of course, we ask them randomly, depending on what we are interested in. This is exactly what you'll do below, fixing this trouble spot. Ask all kinds of questions to every part of the sentence, given here for your training. Please, note that **the rising tone** of voice is used in the **Yes / No and the Tag Questions**, and the **falling tone** has to be used in the **Wh. Questions** - The falling tone should also accentuate the information that is asked in the answer. **Record yourself.**

My brother bought a new computer last week.

1. Yes / No Q.   *Did your brother **buy** a new computer last week?-Yes, he **did**.*

2. Wh. Q. to the subject   ***Who bought** a new computer last week?- **My brother** did.*

3. Wh. Q. to the verb   ***What** did your brother do?- He **bought** a computer.*

4. Wh. Q. to the object   ***What** did your brother buy?- He bought a new computer.*

5. Wh. Q. to an adj.   ***What kind of** computer he buy? - He bought a new computer.*

6. Wh. Q. to the time mod.   *When did he buy a new computer?- He bought it yesterday.*

7. Tag. Q.   *a) Your brother bought a new computer last week, didn't he?*

b) Your brother bought a new computer, right?

c) Your brother bought a new ⌣ computer?

Practice this work with the examples in any tense. For example; *I have sold my house. She will be shopping in the mall tomorrow./ Bob will get a promotion next month. Etc.*

2. There is another great practice for you to consider. Write the same sentence in 5 main tenses, and ask all kinds of questions to all of then, one by one, changing the helping verbs and the main verb forms according to the tense. Here are 5 tense variants of one sentence:

1. I take a shower every day. 2. I took a shower 10 min. ago. 3. I will take a shower in a minute. 4. I am taking a shower now. 5. I have just taken a shower. (Ask all kind of questions to all the five sentences: Yes / No questions, Wh. Questions and Tag questions)

Trouble Spot 3

Simple Writing Skills in Five Main Tenses

In this remedy, we would like you to focus on simple **writing skills about your life in five main tenses**. We will improvise the following mini-essays so you could later adjust them according to your liking and time-management. *(Check with the word- order directions and the remedy on the English sentence structure)*

Only with these two remedies, regularly "taken by you for your English mind" can you write these simple essays correctly, **paying aware attention to** *the word-order, the tenses, the articles, the thought-connectors, and the punctuation*

Also, pay attention to **the brain signals** used in the text. They signify a particular action and make it easier for you to frame your thoughts in a required tense. You just drive your English brain mobile along the mental tracks of the English language, not the native one.

Try to note every comma after the introductory words in a sentence as well as the commas used to separate compound or complex sentences.

Also, mind it, please, that if you start a sentence with a modifier of time or place, you use a comma to show that you are familiar with the English word0order in a sentence which is supposed to start with a subject.

Stay Focused!

1. My Every Day Life - *(the Simple Present Tense);*

2. My Life Yesterday - *(the Simple Past Tense)*

3. My Life Tomorrow - *(the Simple Future Tense0.*

4. My Life at the Moment - (*The Present Progressive Tense)*

5. My Accomplishments today - *(The Present Perfect Tense).*

Space for Notes:

Be Concerned with Understanding
and Being Understood!

Trouble Spot 4

My Every Day Life

1. Please, read this very simple 5 paragraph mini-essay. Then, **write out the highlighted word-combinations in the Infinitive form** on the index cards or into your "My Right Language Behavior" notebook, section "Writing" **in the same logical order** as they come in the text. The word-combinations will serve as the blueprint of the essay. They will channel your thoughts. **Record this text for your reflection on your English first with the text, then without it.**

*I **wake up** at 7am, but I **get up** at about 7;10, or so. I **stretch, get out of bed**, and **say Hello to** a new day. Then I **go to the bathroom**. I, **wash my face, clean my teeth**, and take a shower. **It** normally **takes me** about 10 min. to finish my morning ritual. After that, I **go back** to my bedroom, **make the bed**, and **get dressed**. I also **brush my hair, make-up** a little, and **use some perfume**. I **like wearing** it to brighten up my mood.*

*At 7: 30, I **am ready for** breakfast. I usually **fix my breakfast** myself. It **isn't** anything fancy. I just **have a cup of coffee** with milk and a sandwich. Sometimes, if I am **not in a rush**, I cook an omelet or **have a couple of hard-boiled eggs**. I do not forget **to take a quick look at** the morning news. I **need to be in the picture** as to the weather and the latest news in the world. At 8 sharp, I **am ready** to leave the house. I need **to get to work on time**. I get **to work** by car, I **love driving**. It takes me about half an hour to get to work if **there is no traffic** on the road.*

*My working day **begins** at 9 o'clock I **have a lot of work to do** and different responsibilities to meet. I **am very busy** at work. At noon, I **have a lunch break** for an hour. I usually **go to the cafeteria** downstairs. After lunch, I **get back to work**, and I **continue working till 5 pm**. So, my working day **is over** at that time. I get **back** to my car and **drive back home.***

*I **come home** at about 6 o'clock. I **am very tired**, so, I **take a shower** to wash off the fatigue. At 7 o'clock, I usually have **dinner**. I **cook dinner** myself. Sometimes, I **have a ready-made dinner** from the refrigerator, and I just **microwave** it. Then, I **relax a little** bit on the couch in the living-room.*

In the evening, I watch TV, read books, listen to music, check my e-mails, or socialize with my friends on the Internet I do not stay up late during the week. I need to be fit for work in the morning. So, I go to bed at about 11 o'clock

2. Next, practice the Question-Answer work on the text. Ask the Yes / No questions and the Wh. questions to every part of the text. Conscious makes it perfect!

Space for Notes:

Discipline your Life in English!

Trouble Spot 5

My Life Yesterday

It is a piece of cake to **change the text above to the Simple Past Tense.** All you have to do is to change the verbs to their second forms and use the appropriate brain signals to indicate the past action.

Please note them the word- combinations on the index cards that you have prepared for the text *My Every Day Life"* will help you reconstruct the text in the Simple Past tense both in speaking and in writing. Remember, Past goes after Past in narration! Here we go.

I woke up at 7 o'clock, but I got up at 7; 10 yesterday. I stretched, got out of bed, and said Hello to a new day. Then I went to the bathroom. I washed my face, cleaned my teeth, and took a quick shower. It took me 10 min. to finish my morning ritual After that, I went back to my bedroom, made the bed, and got dressed. I also brushed my hair, made up a little, and used some perfume. I put on the perfume because I wanted to brighten up my day.

At 7; 30, I fixed breakfast myself yesterday. It wasn't anything fancy. I just had a cup of coffee with milk and a sandwich. At breakfast, I watched the TV news to be in the picture as ti the weather and the latest news in the world. At 8 sharp, I left the house. I drove to work. It took me about half an hour to get to work. Since there was no traffic on the road, I managed to get to work on time.

My working day began at 9 o'clock. I had a lot of work to do. I was very busy at work till noon, I had a lunch break for an hour. After lunch, I got back to work, and I kept on working till 5 pm. So, my working day was over at that time. I got back to my car and drove back home.

I came home at about 7 o'clock. I was very tired, so I took a shower to wash off the fatigue. At 7 o'clock, I had dinner. After dinner, I relaxed a little bit on the couch in the living-room.

In the evening, I watched TV, read books, checked my emails, and socialized with my friends on the Internet. I did not go to bed late yesterday. I went to bed at 11 o'clock.

Practice the **Question-Answer work**, too. Try to ask the Yes or No questions and the **Wh. Questions** to every part of the text. Practice makes it perfect!!

Record this text. First read it out, then restore it by its blueprint- the word-combinations that you have written out in a logical order. **Like the way you speak.**

Space for Notes:

Establish a Tight Control over your English!

Trouble Spot 6

My Life Tomorrow

Now, you might want **to transform the same text into the Simple Future Tense.** We'll have to change the brain signals for the future and use the helping verb **will**. The Simple Future Tense is, in fact, the first English Tense with which a new tense structure had been introduced in the English language historically. **The helping verb is** pointing to the grammatical form of a verb, **the main verb** carries the lexical meaning of it. (*Will +1st form*) *Here we go.*

*I **will get up** at 7; 10 tomorrow. First, I **will go to the bathroom**, wash my face, clean my teeth, and take a quick shower. **It will take me** about 10 min. to complete my morning ritual. Then I **will go back** to my bedroom and get dressed. I **will also brush my hair**, make up a little bit, and put on some perfume to brighten up my mood.*

*I **will fix my breakfast** very quickly. It **won't be** anything fancy. I **will just drink a cup of coffee** with milk and eat a sandwich. At breakfast, I **will watch the TV news** to be in the picture as to he weather and the latest news in the world. Then, I **will leave the house,** and I will drive to work. I will not be late to work tomorrow **if I leave** the house at 8 sharp. I **will arrive at work** on time.*

*My working day **will begin** at 9 o'clock. I **will have a lot of work to do**. I will be very busy till noon. At 12 pm, I **will have a lunch break.** After lunch. I **will get back to work**, and I **will stay at work** till 5 pm.*

*Then, I **will go home**. I **will come home** at about 7 pm. I will be pretty tired. So, I **will take a shower** to wash off the fatigue. I **will have dinner** and relax*

*In the evening, I **will watch TV,** read books, listen to music, check my emails, or socialize with my friends on the internet. I **will go to bed** at 11 o'clock tomorrow.*

Please, mind a few important things in this text.

1. You do not need to repeat the helping verb **will** all the time when different actions follow one another.

2. You must not use the Simple Future tense **in the clauses of time and condition** that is, after the words **when** and **if.** E g. I will come to work on time **if** there **is** no traffic on the road.

3. Pay attention that we are not using the conjunction **"And"** at the beginning of the sentence to connect different ideas. Please, do not do that, either! Record yourself. Reflect on your English.

Space for Notes:

Expand your Aware Attention Span!

Trouble Spot 7

My Life at the Present Moment

The Present Progressive tense is the most important tense in our life because it defines our actions at the present moment. Since, according to Albert Einstein, there is no past, no future, just the time as we perceive it in the present, the use of the Present Progressive tense becomes very indicative of the correct use of English. Pay attention to how often people drop the verb "to be" in this tense in casual, communication and use just the present participle of a verb *E.g. I driving, instead of I am driving.* Record yourself. Reflect on your English.

Note, please, that native speakers often drop the helping verb to be in a casual conversation. This language behavior allows for the use of the elliptical English forms in colloquial English. You, however, need to be mindful of this mistake and not to make it mindlessly. Here you go;

I am living in the present, and I am enjoying my life. I love learning English. as a matter of fact, I am working at my English right now. I am trying to reason out some trouble spots in my English. I am thinking in English. I am describing my life in English at this very moment. I am sure, I am doing well. I feel I am becoming better and better in my use of grammar!

Trouble Spot 8

My Accomplishments Today

This text will be written **in the Present Perfect tense** because it is meant **to describe an action in the result for the present.** The Present Perfect tense is often confused with the Simple Past tense because they are translated in the same way. However, the meanings of these two tenses is absolutely different. The Simple Past tense describes a simple past action at a definite time in the past. The Present Perfect tense, though it is translated in the past fashion, means the completion of the action in principle, without any indication when it was done. It's that simple!

---

*I **have done** a lot of things today. I **have done** some shopping, and I **have done** my laundry, too. I **have cooked** dinner. I **have worked** on the computer, and I **have completed** the report that I am supposed to submit on Monday. I **have looked though** many e-mails and I **have responded** to a couple of them. I **have,** actually, **had** a very successful day. I **have accomplished** a lot today, and I am quite happy about it. I have had a happy and resultful day.*

Nothing is Impossible with Good English!

Trouble Spot 9

Manage Your Interviewing Skills

Interviewing skills are part of the package of the holistic display of your Social Intelligence that good knowledge of English is promoting altogether. Below, learn to interview yourself and others. Develop your Cultural Intelligence, too. Get interested in other cultures. Start your explanations with the thought-connector: *The thing is, ...* Record your answers.

1. Getting Americanized

1. To what extent did you get Americanized living in the USA? Prove your point.	
2. Do you like American individualism and privacy? How so?	
3. What part of the American life style have you made yours?	
4. What about a self-help concept? How do you relate to the concept of self-reliance in the USA?	
5. What are the differences between your culture and the American one?	

6. **What do you reject in the American culture? Why?** Specify please.	_____ _____ _____
7. **What would you like to accept in it? Why?** Prove your point.	_____ _____ _____
Conclusion:	_____ _____ _____

2. Getting Adjusted to the International World

1. **How many different cultures did you come in touch with in the USA?** 2. **What is appealing / unacceptable for you in this cultural environment?** Specify please.	_____ _____ _____ _____ _____ _____
3. **How do these cultures impact you?** 4. **What does the concept of the cultural intelligence mean to you?** In what way do you implement it in your life?	_____ _____ _____ _____ _____ _____
5. **Could you marry somebody from an alien culture, or would you rather marry some one from your own country? How so?** Prove your point.	_____ _____ _____ _____

6. **What does it mean to feel international in the USA? Isn't this feeling great? If so, why? Aren't we all getting more and more internationally cultured thanks to the Internet?** Prove your point.	_____ _____ _____ _____ _____ _____
7. **What country would you prefer living in for the rest of your life? How so?** Prove your point.	_____ _____ _____
Conclusion:	_____ _____ _____

3. Making Career Decisions

1. **What type of career are you going to choose? Is this decision life defining?** 2. **How come?**	_____ _____ _____ _____
3. **What can you tell us about an access to education in the U.S.A.? Why do many people from abroad aspire to get to the US colleges?** What's your take on that?	_____ _____ _____ _____ _____ _____
4. **Describe the education system in your country at this moment? What is different in it with the educational system in the USA?**	_____ _____ _____ _____ _____

5. Do you find the American education system to be less demanding and challenging? How so? Specify please.	_____ _____ _____ _____
6. What can you tell us about a student- professor relationship in your country and the USA? What is appealing in it? 7. Is it different in your culture? How so?	_____ _____ _____ _____ _____ _____
Conclusion:	_____ _____ _____

Income Never Exceeds Self-Development!

4. Choosing where to Work

1. What kind of employer do you prefer to have and why? What qualities should a good employer have in your understanding?	_____ _____ _____ _____ _____
2. What is the main thing to choose a work place if you had such a choice? 3. Is it the pay, or the area of expertise that matters? Prove your point please.	_____ _____ _____ _____

4. Would you rather work for a big company or a small one? Why? Prove your point.	_____ _____ _____
5. In what case would you feel confident and professional? What do you know about the atmosphere of synergy at work?	_____ _____ _____ _____ _____
6. Do you trust anybody in helping you with the decision where to work? 7. How important is decision-making in your life? Are you good/ bad at it?	_____ _____ _____ _____ _____
Conclusion:	_____ _____ _____

Before you Get something, Become Someone!

5. Making a Difference in Life

1. What would you like to do in order to change the world? What would you like to change in it? Prove your point.	_____ _____ _____
2. Do you really believe than one person can make a difference in this world? How so?	_____ _____

3. **Do you have courage to start a project on your own? Which one?**	_____ _____ _____
4. **Do you have enough self-esteem to lead a group? Why yes or why not?**	_____ _____ _____
5. **Does one really need a goal in life to make a difference in it? What does the concept of self-expression mean to you?**	_____ _____ _____ _____
6. **Does speaking correct English make a difference in your professional life? Prove your point.**	_____ _____ _____ _____

Continue the Quest for Being the Best!

Boost your Brain Power with Conscious Learning!

English is Ruling the World!

You are Ruling Your English!

Section 2

The Final Display Of Knowledge Awareness And Self-Assessment Skills

Questionnaire

It's Easier to Learn any Language Right Than to relearn it again and again!

1. Holistic Picture of You in the Language

In the introduction to this book, we pointed out how important it is for you to **stop seeing yourself in the language and start seeing the language in you**. Feeling in the language is associated with being too self-conscious, fearful to make mistakes in a foreign language, shy, confused, not totally yourself since the power of self-expression is limited. Please, tell us in general terms and most sincerely how you feel about your socializing in English. Please feel free to get in touch with us on the website to help you better diagnose your English to help you out with any issue. Mind Albert Einstein's words at the bottom of this page!

1. Use these word: **less/ more confused; / still / less lost; / more / less fluent; / more / less confident; more / less tongue-tied; more / less comfortable with ...; more / less conscious of the incorrect English in m;, more / less language-disciplined...etc.**

2. How does incorrect / more correct use of English affect your feelings now?

Specify, please: _____
_____
_____
_____

2. Final Holistic Assessment

On the scale of 0 to 10, assess your Language Habits and Speech Skills.

Language Habits

a) Pronunciation. Habits - E.g. (7)

1. Do you feel more / less confident about the way you sound in English? Specify please.

_____

_____

_____

b) Grammatical Habits - (6)

1. What grammar structures, phenomena have you managed to clarify for yourself?

_____

_____

_____

2. Do you feel more competent in the language? Specify please.

_____

_____

_____

c) Vocabulary Habits - ( )

Do you think that working on the vocabulary enriching tips helped you?- How so?

_____

_____

_____

"Awareness is always the first Step to Progress!"

Speech Skills

a) Listening Skills - ( )

1. Do you understand spoken English better?

_____

_____

_____

2. What helps your oral communication most?

_____

_____

_____

3. What tips on bettering your listening skills work most for you?

_____

_____

_____

b) Speaking Skills - ( )

1. Do you feel fess tongue- tired in face-to face communication? Which of our remedies worked best for you?

_____

_____

_____

c) Reading Skills - ( )

1. If your reading comprehension better now? Thanks to what? What remedies on reading work best for you?

_____

_____

_____

d) Writing Skills - (   )

1. Do you have a better idea how to perfect your writing in English? Which remedies work best for you?

_____

_____

_____

Space for Notes:

Bettering the language, you better yourself!

3. Your Second Language Personality

1. How can you qualify your personal powers when you communicate in English? Why do you feel more confident if your speak / write in English correctly?

_____

_____

_____

2. What changes do you experience **personality-wise**, living in English" professionally, socially, personally?

_____

_____

_____

3. Do you experience much **difference in your thinking sk**ills in English?

_____

_____

_____

4. Has your thinking in English become less native language entangled? Is it **conscious / unconscious** now?

_____

_____

_____

5. How does thinking in English and speaking it more fluently **change your perception of** life in general?

_____

_____

_____

6. If you are currently living / studying in the USA, to do you **feel, think, act differently** ? How so?

_____

_____

_____

7. Do you feel that you are **getting a little / much more Americanize culture-w**ise? How does such thinking, impact you behavior, your cultural values, your social skill?

_____

_____

_____

7. How does the saying, **"Life is tough, but I am tougher"** apply to you?

_____

_____

_____

8. How do the words **"God bless America!"** resonate with you?

_____

_____

_____

Space for Notes:

Train Your Brain!

End of Part 4 "Impeccable English"

English is Ruling the World!

You are Ruling Your English!

The Code
Of
The Right Language
Behavior

Develop Your Second Language Personality!

Control your English or English will control You!

1. Vistas of General Intelligence

In conclusion, let's get back to the cones of **language-speech evolution**, presented in the goals 2 and 3, as your top goals in Book One. Both goals are focused on your obtaining a new language consciousness that starts developing at the first level of a language learning odyssey, the micro level and brings you up to new mental abilities, **a new language consciousness formation.** As the process of language learning develops from the **Mini, Meta, Mezzo** levels to the **Macro** and **Super** one, we, accordingly, deal with **the levels of general intelligence** that language use and language perfection in terms of the right language behavior are propelling in you. This is **an integrated web of intelligences** that are being developed on the basis of your language intelligence and help you **get integrated into the new, technology-based, social intelligence.**

The Levels of General Intelligence Development

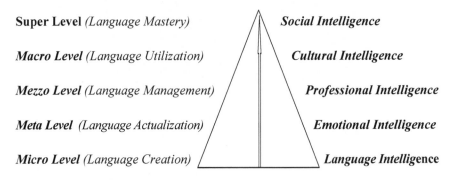

Super Level *(Language Mastery)*   *Social Intelligence*

Macro Level (Language Utilization)   *Cultural Intelligence*

Mezzo Level (Language Management)   *Professional Intelligence*

Meta Level (Language Actualization)   *Emotional Intelligence*

Micro Level (Language Creation)   *Language Intelligence*

Language intelligence is at the basis of your general intelligence that incorporates your language/ speech competence that helps you articulate you intelligent needs, be argumentative, think critically, and promote your ideas.

Emotional intelligence helps you monitor your feelings in the second language, and it raises your intellectual set-point to a new level of intelligence.

Professional intelligence is your operational intelligence in life, your business intelligence. It helps you continuously improve your professional skills.

Cultural intelligence helps you in a dynamic interchange among cultures. Recent trends, including high-tech communication are cresting new challenges for global interaction. You also need to expand your knowledge base in art. Literature, science to be a well- cultured person that fits perfectly in the fast changing world.

Social intelligence is the one that engages you in the present day social networking and takes you to a new level of social interaction in which the role of English is dominant.

Space for Notes:

Raise Your General Intelligence!

2. Super Language - Speech Dimension!

So, the study of a second language is to embark upon a journey of self-development, self-discovery, self-actualization, and self-realization in the present day world. As a matter of fact, alongside with the structural (language habits) and communicative (speech skills) goals that acquiring any foreign language has, this is also the process of **a deep physiological change.** It is the process of a transformation into another mind-set and another cultural frame-work. Since you step into a new language personality role, we will help you mold this role to your personal psychological frame-work.

Any foreign language learning is a great mental and psychological job when a learner is **reaching out to new thinking dimensions,** changing his/her intellectual landscape entirely and building up a new language mentality. With language taking deeper rooting in the brain, you **integrate the English language personality values** into your basic character-framework and your life actualization. The ground issue here is that every individual has to consciously take responsibility for his language, be it a native language or a foreign one. Here comes the most important issue in the formation of a second language personality. It is the development of your second language awareness that we tried to deepen with this book.

A great American linguist, John Ausbell, was right, but too much ahead of his time when in 1960, he wrote, **"Adults, learning a second language must do it consciously, making use of their native language awareness"** And it is the native language awareness that needs to be much better installed in the learners' brains at school. Native language awareness paves the way to the second one, and it puts an end to automatic, mindless speaking and writing. We need to teach our kids to expand their language horizons beyond the habitual ways of seeing, listening, and speaking. General language awareness catalyzes the process of language use and helps a language learner / user find the key to maintaining his / her language-speech equilibrium, based on a solid respect for the language of communication and a newly found self-respect.

For the next several months, your job is **to invest 15 to 20 minutes a day, reading and rereading the book,** memorizing and practicing the operational tools that we offer here. Get deeper and deeper interested in the recommendations that we provide and apply the remedies to your every day speaking / writing in English. You should carry the set of cards that you have prepared going through the pages of this book with you everywhere. Check them out. Let them remind you to keep control over your English every walking, talking, eating, and listening moment. Momentum builds. A new self-image will emerge and it will empower you to walk out of your old SL history and walk into your language future. Living is learning, and learning is living!

Space for Notes:

Good luck on your Language-Speech Odyssey!

3. Master Emotional Diplomacy!

Summing up our work on the book, we need to emphasize the importance of **emotional intelligence** in the second language operation again. It is, in fact, **the synchronicity of mind and emotions** in operating the second language. It is a big challenge for the native language speakers, to begin with, and this is the goal that all of us have to accomplish.

Learning a foreign/ second language is truly a journey. The road has its ups and downs. That is why building up your personal stamina is a crucial part of the remedial process because you along side with changing your mental landscape in the brain, you are altering the emotional one, too. You are fortifying your emotional intelligence in English that is being formulated with each mistake that you correct and the emotional turmoil that you beat in the bud with your right language behavior.

Negative thoughts about you in the language stop grabbing hold of your attention like a powerful magnet and you get out of the loop of fear and insecurity. **You stop feeling yourself in the language and start felling the language in you!** Self-boosters at the bottom of each page are a great way to give your psyche a back- up and your brain an emotional energizer. You need to help yourself emotionally to master a foreign language. Emotional intelligence is at work here.

The method of the Conscious Language Behavior is, actually, building the living intelligence in the language. By living intelligence we mean the state of deep consciousness and mental clarity in the language. Anything unconscious dissolves when you shine the light of consciousness on it! So, you need to step out of your relative, mechanical, emotional hullabaloo, knowledge of the language and start enjoying the conscious, operative, and optimal state of your language / speech competence. Very soon, you will have an inspiring sensation of your new feeling of the language and a new self-image. Actually, **the greatest benefit of a foreign language speaking is feeling good about oneself!**

Step out on the stage of your mind to practice the language consciously! Only conscious mind is responsible for the verbal expression. Only conscious mind removes the self-inhibition and helps you establish the self-evaluation of the rightness or wrongness of the language actions you are about to implement. **Language becomes inwardly controllable.** As a result, you will feel much more confident in communication because you have consciously removed the language imperfections that inhibited your second language personality growth. That's the outcome of our work, and we hope you feel more accomplished in English than before it won't hurt to go over some parts pf the book again, and we are there for you on the website.

Space for Notes:

Fix the Inner language, better the Outer speech!

4. Don't be Lazy to Think!

"The brain has to be trained, but the mind has to be discovered" These wonderful words belong to a brain researcher Osho, and they excellently convey the master message of this book. We think that lacking individual mental channeling in language learning leads to an individual fully developed into a loafer, as he /she needs not to think but accept information without judgment. Such situations develop language cripples when language is converted into mechanical speech that fossilizes the bad language habits in the brain. A student is within his mental eggshell. Therefore, it's so hard for him/ her to produce any argument, reasoning, or the facts that may oblige him to think. The student is still in the cubicle mental space of his native language. But you have cured this situation for yourself. Your goal is this book is to change the way you think in English, and you have accomplished this goal. Congratulations!

We have injected some language awareness into that cubicle to generate low or higher speech vibrations to identify the neural correlation between language and speech that are out of synch. Apparently, **training thinking skills has to be a priority in language learning** or language remedying. You need to develop your thinking skills every moment of the second language use, Don't be lazy to think in English!. Don't leave your language remedying work to the charm of the compliment, "You English is cute". Don't lull your brain to deny the reality. Keep learning!

Every new language is a change of the intellectual landscape in the brain. Each cell in the brain is a micro-processor linked to billions of other. Brain cells give rise to brain waves that emit information through the network of neurons. A good proof to the necessity to develop the thinking skills, be it in the native language or a foreign one, is the study of Albert Einstein's unique brain that had taken three years to be completed. His brain cells were counted to see what made his brain capacity different.

It was discovered that **Albert Einstein had 27% more thinking cells** in the brain than an average human being. The difference is in the quality of his cells, not in their quantity. Einstein had more thinking cells that grew because he did his conscious thinking non-stop. Both of his theories of relativity were born in his **thinking laboratory**, in his hard-working mind. Unfortunately, the present day teaching system stupefies students. That which is intellect-charged appears to be so unattractive that no one bothers to study it or make an effort to delve beneath the surface. So, teaching yourself to think in English is an absolute necessity! When you start thinking in English, you start **becoming a new language individuality**, which grows into **a** Second Language Personality. This book provides the modus operandi, the hierarchy of the operative forces in language remedying, and we are happy that you can benefit by using it to become a better thinker in English.**"Consciousness is the blueprint of everything!"**

Space for Notes:

Thinking in English is your Ultimate Goal!

5. Second Language Personality Growth

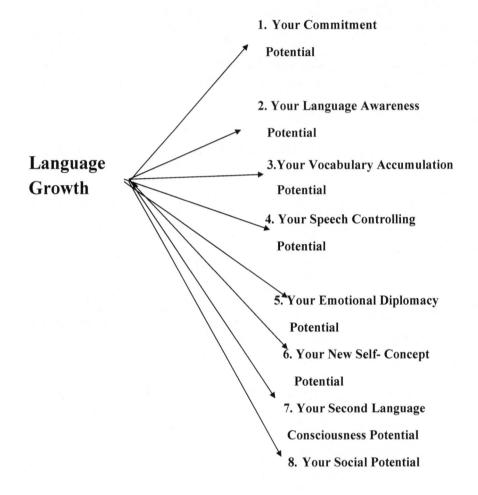

Language Growth

1. Your Commitment Potential

2. Your Language Awareness Potential

3.Your Vocabulary Accumulation Potential

4. Your Speech Controlling Potential

5. Your Emotional Diplomacy Potential

6. Your New Self- Concept Potential

7. Your Second Language Consciousness Potential

8. Your Social Potential

A New Language is a new Language Personality!

6. The Code of the Right Language Behavior

1. Reprogram and recondition your mind for **the correct language behavior**. That is, walk out of your old SL history and start building a new one. If you want to improve the quality of your English, improve your personality in it first. Strengthen your self-image **Move from a subjective vision of yourself in the language to an objective vision of the language in you!**

2. Study the **Language Management Rules** Instill the zest for **disciplined learning** in yourself.

3. The power of learning English is the process of destroying the walls of resistance:

a) The national wall; b) the material wall; c) the mental wall; d) the psychological wall

4. **Establish a zealous control over your thinking, speaking, and writing in English!** Learn to put the spotlight of your attention on the language structure. Feel its power in you to energize your speech. Be courteous, tactful, and respectful! **"Raise your words, not voice!** "*(Rumi)*

5. **Say No to mechanical speaking /writing**! Have a constructive approach to your mistakes. Be conscious of them in the speech of others as well.

6. **Feel the right to correct yourself** and take time to do that. Better speak slowly, but correctly. Learn to hear out the other person.

7. The sense of fear to say something wrong has to be eradicated first. **No language victim mentality!** Feel free to say, Sorry, I didn't get you. Could you kindly repeat it?

8. **Put** the letter "T" before the letter "S" and "W." **Think before speaking / writing!**

9. **Correct speaking generates correct writing**. Pay aware attention to what you are writing. Don't lose the train of your thought. Stay focused. Writing is the passport of your mind.

10. **Discriminate between the rules of speaking and writing**. They are different!

11 **Develop your language intuition** every speaking / writing moment. Don't be sloppy in your wording. Get rid of the junk words. Don't stigmatize your English!

12. The formation of **a Second Language Personality** is a long process of challenge and result, not an overnight destination. A new language personality is a new language mentality.

13. **Be proud of yourself in English and make it proud of you in reverse.** Let your language exposure be oriented on the successful ultimate result that helps you shine in your life.

Stay Connected!

7. Focus on the Art of Becoming!

Some one said, **"Education is the process of discovering your own ignorance"** We say:

It may be very

    True

Education is our lives'

    Guru

        So, educate your mind-

        Set

        At every mental

        Step!

Never worry what

    To do,

Make the time for your brain's

    Guru

        Read, listen, and in-

        spire,

        Perceive all that's there to ac-

        quire

To never be a

    Bore

And to learn much, much

    More!

"If it's to be, it's up to me!"

English is Ruling the World!

You are Ruling Your English!

The Appendix

Some Helpful Stuff At Hand

Bettering Your English is a Life-Long Commitment!

1. Associative Groups of Verbs

Here are **the mostly used English verbs, systematized into the groups by their common meaning.** They are presented in the 4 forms to make it easier for you to use them in different tense forms. The irregular verbs are highlighted.

Associative Groups of Verbs	INF	I FORM	II FORM	III FORM (P.P)	IV -ING FORM
# Verb Meanings:	TO	SIMPLE PRESENT	SIMPLE PAST	PAST PARTICIPLE	PRESENT PARTICIPLE
1 FUNDA-MENTALS	to to to to	- am **be - are** - is **have(has)** **do (does)** **get(s)**	**was were** **had** **done** **got**	**been** **had** **done** **gotten**	being having doing getting
2 SPEECH	to to to to	**speak (s)** **say(s)** **tell (s) sb.** talk (s) to	**spoke** **said** **told** talked	**spoken** **said** **told** talked	speaking saying telling talking
3 CONVER-SATION	to to to to to to	ask answer repeat reply discuss respond	asked answered repeated replied discussed responded	asked answered repeated replied discussed responded	asking answering repeating replying discussing responding
4 MEANING	to to to to to	**mean** express imply conclude infer	**meant** expressed implied concluded inferred	**meant** expressed implied concluded inferred	**meaning** expressing implying concluding inferring
5 MIND	to to to to	**think** guess **understand** **know**	**thought** guessed **understood** **knew**	**thought** guessed **understood** **known**	thinking guessing understanding knowing

		to	remember	remembered	remembered	remembering
6	MEMORY	to	**forget**	**forgot**	**forgotten**	forgetting
		to	recall	recalled	recalled	recalling
7	OPINION	to	believe	believed	believed	believing
		to	**mean**	**meant**	**meant**	meaning
		to	consider	considered	considered	considering
8	IDEAS	to	suggest	suggested	suggested	suggesting
		to	recommend	recommended	recommended	recommending
		to	advise	advised	advised	advising
9	VISION	to	**see**	**saw**	**seen**	seeing
		to	look (at)	looked	looked	looking
		to	watch	watched	watched	watching
		to	notice	noticed	noticed	noticing
		to	visualize	visualized	visualized	visualizing
		to	imagine	imagined	imagined	imagining
10	THE VERBS OF ACTION	*to*	**give**	**gave**	**given**	giving
		to	**take**	**took**	**taken**	taking
		to	**put**	**Put**	**Put**	putting
		to	pull	pulled	pulled	pulling
		to	**bring**	**brought**	**brought**	bringing
		to	push	pushed	pushed	pushing
		to	**make**	**made**	**made**	making
		to	practice	practiced	practiced	practicing
11	HEARING	to	**hear**	**heard**	**heard**	**hearing**
		to	listen (to)	listened	listened	listening
		to	hear sb. out	Heard sb. out	Heard sb. out	hearing
12	SENSATION	to	**feel**	**felt**	**felt**	feeling
		to	sense	sensed	sensed	sensing
		to	**smell**	**smelt**	**smelt**	Smelling
		to	taste	tasted	tasted	tasting
		to	touch	touched	touched	touching
13	NEEDS	to	**eat**	**ate**	**eaten**	eating
		to	**drink**	**drank**	**drunk**	drinking
		to	breathe	breathed	breathed	breathing
		to	**sleep**	**slept**	**slept**	sleeping
14	WISH	to	want	wanted	wanted	wanting
		to	wish	wished	wished	wishing
		to	desire	desired	desired	desiring
		to	long	longed	longed	longing

15	**THE VERBS OF MOVEMENT**	to to to to to to	**go** **come** move arrive **leave** **drive**	**went** **came** moved arrived **left** **drove**	**gone** **come** moved arrived **left** **driven**	going coming Moving arriving leaving driving
16	**REST**	to to to	rest relax loosen	rested relaxed loosened up	rested relaxed loosened up	resting relaxing loosening
17	**SKILLS**	to to to to to to to	**read** **write** **draw** count dance **sing** perform	**read** **wrote** **drew** counted danced **sang** performed	**read** **written** **drawn** counted danced **sung** performed	reading writing drawing counting dancing singing performing
18	**LIKING**	to to to to	like love care (for) prefer	liked loved cared preferred	liked loved cared preferred	liking loving caring preferring
19	**DISLIKING**	to to to to	hate dislike ignore disregard	hated disliked ignored disregarded	hated disliked ignored disregarded	hating disliking ignoring disregarding
20	**THE VERBS OF SCHOOLING**	to to to to	study **learn** **teach** instruct	studied **learnt** **taught** instructed	studied **learnt** **taught** instructed	studying learning teaching instructing
21	**STARTING**	to to to	start **begin** commence	started **began** commenced	started **begun** commenced	starting beginning commencing
22	**CONTINUING**	to to to	continue **go on** proceed	continued **went on** proceeded	continued **gone on** proceeded	continuing going on proceeding
23	**FINISHING**	to to to	finish stop discontinue	finished stopped discontinued	finished stopped discontinued	finishing stopping discontinuing

		to	save	saved	saved	saving
24	**MONEY**	to	owe	owed	owed	owing
	MATTERS	to	borrow	borrowed	borrowed	borrowing
		to	Lend	lent	lent	lending
		to	**cost**	**cost**	**cost**	costing
25	**SHOPPING**	to	**buy**	**bought**	**bought**	buying
		to	**pay**	**paid**	**paid**	paying
		to	exchange	exchanged	exchanged	exchanging
		to	**sell**	**sold**	**sold**	selling
		to	shop	shopped	shopped	hopping
		to	discount	discounted	discounted	discounting
		to	deposit	deposited	deposited	depositing
26	**THE VERBS**	to	**withdraw**	**withdrew**	**withdrawn**	withdrawing
	OF	to	invest	invested	invested	investing
	BANKING	to	indorse	indorsed	indorsed	indorsing
		to	pass	passed	passed	passing
27	**ACADEMIC**	to	fail	failed	failed	failing
	LIFE	to	expel	expelled	expelled	expelling
		to	minor	minored	minored	minoring
28	**MAJORING**	to	transfer	transferred	transferred	transferring
	IN	to	major	majored	majored	majoring
	A SUBJECT	to	quiz	quizzed	quizzed	quizzing
		to	rent	rented	rented	renting
29	**RENTING**	to	lease	leased	leased	leasing
		to	sublease	subleased	subleased	subleasing
		to	wait (for)	waited	waited	waiting
30	**EXPECTA-**	to	expect	expected	expected	expecting
	TION	to	hope	hoped	hoped	hoping
		to	call	called	called	calling
31	**TELEPHONE**	to	phone	phoned	phoned	phoning
		to	dial	dialed	dialed	dialing
		to	**hold on**	**held on**	**held on**	holding on
		to	**hang up**	**hung up**	**hung up**	hanging up
		to	**ring**	**rang**	**rung**	ringing

		to	attain	attained	attained	attaining
32	SUCCESS	to	manage	managed	managed	managing
		to	succeed	succeeded	succeeded	succeeding
		to	gain	gained	gained	gaining
		to	achieve	achieved	achieved	achieving
		to	accomplish	accomplished	accomplished	accomplishing
33	FAILURE	to	fail	failed	failed	failing
		to	mess up	messed up	messed up	messing up
		to	**lose**	**lost**	**lost**	losing
		to	ruin	ruined	ruined	ruining
		to	destroy	destroyed	destroyed	destroying
		to	screw	screwed	screwed	screwing
34	HELP	to	provide	provided	provided	providing
		to	help	helped	helped	helping
		to	aid	aided	aided	aiding
		to	assist	assisted	assisted	assisting
35	MEETING	to	**meet**	**met**	**met**	meeting
		to	greet	greeted	greeted	greeting
		to	part	parted	parted	parting
36	SEARCHING	to	Search	searched	searched	searching
		to	Look for	looked	looked	looking
		to	**find**	**found**	**found**	finding
		to	**seek**	**sought**	**sought**	seeking
37	THE VERBS OF DATING	to	date	dated	dated	dating
		to	court	courted	courted	courting
		to	**go out**	**went out**	**gone out**	going out
38	ILLS	to	**hurt**	**hurt**	**hurt**	hurting
		to	treat	treated	treated	treating
		to	heal	healed	healed	healed
		to	cure	cured	cured	curing
39	GESTURES	to	point (at)	pointed	pointed	pointing
		to	Show	Showed	Showed	Showing
		to	Hand (in)	Handed	Handed	Handing
		to	Wave	Waved	Waved	Waving
40	WASHING	to	Clean	Cleaned	Cleaned	Cleaning
		to	Wash	Washed	Washed	Washing
		to	Remove	Removed	Removed	Removing
		to	scrub	scrubbed	scrubbed	scrubbing

		to	take off	took off	taken off	taking off
41	CLOTHING	to	put on	put on	put on	putting
		to	wear	wore	worn	wearing
		to	dress	dressed	dressed	dressing
42	EMPLOY-MENT	to	work	worked	worked	working
		to	employ	employed	employed	employing
		to	hire	hired	hired	hiring
		to	fire	fired	fired	firing
		to	interview	interviewed	interviewed	interviewing
43	BODY MOVEMENTS	to	sit	Sat	Sat	sitting
		to	stand	stood	stood	standing
		to	fall	fell	fallen	falling
		to	lie	lay	lain	lying
		to	rise	rose	risen	rising
		to	run	ran	run	running
		to	dance	danced	danced	dancing
		to	raise	raised	raised	raising
		to	jump	jumped	jumped	jumping
44	POSITIVE EMOTIONS	to	smile	smiled	smiled	smiling
		to	laugh	laughed	laughed	laughing
		to	kiss	kissed	kissed	kissing
		to	hug	hugged	hugged	hugging
		to	embrace	embraced	embraced	embracing
45	NEGATIVE EMOTIONS	to	cry	cried	cried	crying
		to	shout	shouted	shouted	shouted
		to	yell (at)	yelled	yelled	yelling
		to	argue	argued	argued	arguing
		to	insult	insulted	insulted	insulting
46	FIGHTING	to	fight	fought	fought	fighting
		to	hit	hit	hit	hitting
		to	attack	attacked	attacked	attacking
		to	beat	beat	beaten	beating
		to	strike	struck	struck	striking
47	TRANSPORTA-TION	to	drive	drove	driven	driving
		to	ride	rode	ridden	riding
		to	fly	flew	flown	flying
		to	sail	sailed	sailed	sailing
		to	swim	swam	swum	swimming
		to	commute	commuted	commuted	commuting

48	WORK ISSUES	to to to to to to	hire fire employ cash utilize use	hired fired employed cashed utilized used	hired fired employed cashed utilized used	hiring firing employing cashing utilizing using
49	POSSESSION	to to to to	belong (to) own possess inherit	belonged owned possessed inherited	belonged owned possessed inherited	belonging owning possessing inheriting
50	CLEANING	to to to to	dust **sweep** mop polish	dusted **swept** mopped polished	dusted **swept** mopped polished	dusting sweeping mopping polishing
51	LIGHT	to to to to	turn on turn off darken lighten	turned on turned off darkened lightened	turned on turned off darkened lightened	turning on turned off darkening lightening
52	CHOICE	to to to	**choose** pick select	**chose** picked selected	**chosen** picked selected	choosing picking selecting
53	GRATITUDE	to to to	thank appreciate value	thanked appreciated valued	thanked appreciated valued	thanking appreciating valuing
54	PROMISE	to to to to	promise **forget** **forgive** commit	promised **forgot** **forgave** committed	promised **forgotten** **forgiven** committed	promising forgetting forgiving committing
55	HAPPENING	to to to	happen occur **take place**	happened occurred **took place**	happened occurred **taken place**	happening occurring taking place
56	TRAVELING	to to	travel journey	traveled journeyed	traveled journeyed	traveling journeying
57	TECHNOLOGY	to to to to to	invent develop equip design download	invented developed equipped designed downloaded	invented developed equipped designed downloaded	inventing developing equipping designing downloading

58	**JUDGMENT**	to to to to	judge support back up punish	judged supported backed up punished	judged supported backed up punished	judging supporting backing up punishing
59	**INSULT**	to to to to to	insult **hurt** curse (at) ignore humiliate	insulted **hurt** cursed ignored humiliated	insulted **hurt** cursed ignored humiliated	insulting Hurting cursing ignoring humiliating
60	**PRIORITIES**	to to to to to	prioritize sort of discipline organize arrange	prioritized sorted of disciplined organized arranged	prioritize sorted of disciplined organized arranged	prioritizing sorting of disciplining organizing arranging
61	**COMPARISON**	To To To	Compare Contrast favor	Compared Contrasted favored	Compared Contrasted favored	Comparing Contrasting favoring
62	**SOUNDS**	To To to To	**ring** knock mutter chime	**rang** knocked muttered chimed	**rung** knocked muttered chimed	ringing knocking muttering chiming
63	**SURPRISE**	to to to to to to to	surprise amaze astonish shock bewilder confuse astound	surprised amazed astonished shocked bewildered confused astounded	surprised amazed astonished shocked bewildered confused astounded	surprising amazing astonishing shocking bewildering confusing astounding
64	**THE VERBS OF BODILY FUNCTIONS**	to to to to to to to	breathe inhale exhale urinate pee defecate perspire	breathed inhaled exhaled urinated peed defecated perspired	breathed inhaled exhaled urinated peed defecated perspired	breathing inhaling exhaling urinating peeing defecating perspiring
65	**HOPE**	to to to to	hope believe aspire desire	hoped believed aspired desired	hoped believed aspired desired	hopping believing aspiring desiring

		to	live	lived	lived	living
66	**LIFE**	to	exist	existed	existed	existing
		to	reside	resided	resided	residing
		to	inhabit	inhabited	inhabited	inhabiting
		to	die	died	died	dying
67	**DEATH**	to	pass away	passed away	passed away	passing away
		to	perish	perished	perished	perishing
		to	rejoice	rejoiced	rejoiced	rejoicing
68	**POSITIVE**	to	**forgive**	**forgave**	**forgiven**	forgiving
	THINKING	to	relax	relaxed	relaxed	relaxing
		to	enlighten	enlightened	enlightened	enlightening
		to	empower	empowered	empowered	empowering
		to	enjoy	enjoyed	enjoyed	enjoying

Space for Notes:

2. Popular Verbs, ending in … "ize"

	Verb, ending in …ize	Enrich your speaking and writing with the verbs, ending in IZE They happen to be very handy lately. They are presented in the alphabetic order below. Make up your own examples, too.
	A	
1	**Advertise**	The company **advertised** its product on television
2	**Actualize**	We need **to actualize** the deal we've agreed upon
3	**Aromatize**	She has **aromatized** her freshly done laundry.
4	**Agonize**	She **antagonizes** her neighbors by playing her music too loudly
5	**Attitudinize**	You have **to attitudinize** your behavior in a proper way
6	**Alphabetize**	I need **to alphabetize** the names of the students in my group
7	**Americanize**	My English got pretty much **Americanized** in the USA
8	**Amortize**	We **amortized** our $30,00 loan into $300 per month for several years
9	**Analyze**	I need **to analyze** the situation that we got in.
10	**Antagonize**	He **antagonized** a lot before taking that job
11	**Apologize**	I **apologize** for being rude to you last time.
12	**Authorize**	Congress **authorizes** the government to tax the people

B	
13	**Baptize**	The newly born child **was baptized** in the Catholic church.
14	**Bi-lingualize**	Many kids from the immigrant families **get bi-lingualized** in the USA.
15	**Bureaucratize**	The present day society is extremely **bureaucratized.**
C	
16	**Canonize**	Many godly people **were canonized** as saints by the church.
17	**Capitalize**	We need **to capitalize** on our main goals
18	**Categorize**	I can **categorize** the company's problems as financial.
19	**Centralize**	The management of any company **is** always **centralized**
20	**Civilize**	Good education **civilizes** people
21	**Customize**	The new car **was customized** to my needs.
22	**Contextualize**	It is important for your language skills to learn **to contextualize** new vocabulary units
23	**Customize**	The company **customizes** kitchens the way you want them
24	**Crystallize**	My wish to become an artist **has** never **crystallized**
25	**Compromise**	We need to learn **to compromise** in a relationship.
26	**Characterize**	I cannot **characterize** the behavior of that child.
27	**Criticize**	His article **was** strongly **criticized** by the public.

D	
28	**Decolonize**	Many African countries **were decolonized** in the 19ᵗʰ century
29	**Decentralize**	The work of the company **got decentralized** due to the storm.
30	**Dramatize**	Try to stay calm and **not dramatize** the situation.
31	**Denationalize**	Many African countries **denationalized** many of their plants
32	**Deodorize**	The cleaning woman **deodorized** the bathroom
33	**Departmentalize**	The store was completely **departmentalized.**
34	**Depersonalize**	Many companies **have** completely **depersonalized** their services
35	**Depoliticize**	The President **depoliticized** women's issues
36	**Destabilize**	The world situation **was destabilized** by the Sep.11, 2001 events.
37	**Digitize**	Some thermometers show a **digitized** reading of temperature.
38	**Depolarize**	The presidential race **depolarized** the country's population.
39	**Demagnetize**	She **demagnetizes** the pressure in the room with her kind words.
E	
40	**Economize**	I was broke and had **to economize** every penny.
42	**Equalize**	The mother **equalized** the patrons of food for the children

43	Acclimatize	I cannot **get acclimatized** in the hot weather of Florida.
44	Equalize	She **equalized** her weight with her rival's weight.
45	Emotionalize	She needed **to emotionalize** her performance on stage.
46	Energize	The teacher **energized** the class with his enthusiasm
47	Emphasize	The father **emphasized** the need to reduce the family's expenses.
F		
48	Familiarize	I had to **familiarize** myself with my new job duties
49	Fantasize	She **fantasizes** that she is a famous singer.
50	Finalize	They **finalized** the negations by signing the contract.
51	Feminize	Gay men get **feminized** in their behavior.
52	Fragmentize	The job amount seemed to be huge so, I fragmentized my work
G		
53	Generalize	I **generalized** all the issues that we had discussed at the meeting
54	Galvanize	The politician's ideas **galvanized** the opposition to act against him
55	Glamorize	Newspapers **glamorize** the lives of movie stars
56	Globalize	The internet **globalized** human communication

	H	
57	**Harmonize**	She dressed nicely and **harmonized** her colors well.
58	**Hypnotize**	The therapist **hypnotized** her patient against her drug addiction.
59	**Homogenize**	The milk **is homogenized** so that the cream is mixed evenly
60	**Hospitalize**	She **was hospitalized** for appendicitis.
61	**Humanize**	People **are humanized** by becoming more spiritual.
	I	
61	**Idealize**	She blindly. **idealized** her first husband
62	**Internalize**	The flu shot is meant **to immunize** a body against flue germs
63	**Intellectualize**	We need **to intellectualize** our education goals
64	**Individualize**	The company **individualizes** its services for each customer
65	**Industrialize**	Many developing countries wish **to industrialize** their economies
	J	
66	**Jeopardize**	She **jeopardized** the blanket for the king size bed
	K	
67	**King size**	They **king sized** the blanket for the king size bed

L	
68	**Legalize** — The right for speech **was** finally **legalized** in Russia.
69	**Localize** — Police **localized** the rio.
70	**Legitimize** — By getting married, the couple **legitimized** their little child
71	**Liberalize** — The tax law **was liberalized** to make it easier

M	
72	**Magnetize** — The microcells have **to be magnetized** to become visible for research
73	**Memorize** — Actors have **to memorize** their lines.
74	**Minimize** — The damage **was minimized** by the lawyer.
75	**Maximize** — The company **maximized** their profits
76	**Mobilize** — I need **to mobilize** my strength against the sickness
77	**Monopolize** — Don't **monopolize** the discussion, please
78	**Mesmerize** — The birds in the tree **mesmerized** the cat and me

N	
79	**Normalize** — The leaders met **to normalize** relations between the two countries
80	**Nationalize** — Many banks **were nationalized** in Russia.
81	**Notarize** — I had my signature **notarized.**

O	
82	**Optimize**	The government tried **to optimize** the hardships of the population.
83	**Organize**	We **organized** the work of the business in the best way possible.
84	**Oxidize**	Having long walks outside oxidizes your body

P	
85	**Patronize**	I hate **being patronized** when I am weak and life beaten
86	**Paralyze**	The traffic **was paralyzed** by the accident
87	**Penalize**	We are always **penalized** for not paying the bills on time
88	**Prioritize**	I always **prioritize the objectives of my job.**
89	**Pressurize**	The airplane cabin **has been pressurized,** so you won't get a headache
90	**Plagiarize**	Students must not **plagiarize** other people's work.
91	**Popularize**	The USA **popularized** the wearing of jeans around the world.
92	**Publicize**	Every wrong doing of any celebrity **is** immediately **publicized.**
93	**Polarize**	The fight between the political parties **has polarized** the public

Q	
94	**Queen-size**	A **queen-sized** bed is bigger than a single bed

	R	
95	**Realize**	Government actions made us **realize** their true intentions
96	**Revitalize**	The company **revitalized** the production of steel
97	**Rationalize**	The school **rationalized** its schedule
98	**Reorganize**	Our company **was** completely **reorganized.**
99	**Revolutionize**	Discovery of electricity **revolutionized** the way people lived.
100	S	
1	**Stabilize**	Her health **stabilizes** when she gets her medicine.
2	**Scrutinize**	Every mistake I made at my job **was scrutinized** by my boss.
3	**Spiritualize**	We need **to spiritualize** our lives to become better people.
4	**Socialize**	The internet **has socialized** our life.
5	**Summarize**	I need **to summarize** the ideas presented at the meeting.
6	**Standardize**	We have to standardize the rules of the game
7	**Symbolize**	The Statue of Liberty **symbolizes** the USA
	T	
8	**Traumatize**	Her feelings **were traumatized** by the September 11,2001 events.
9	**Traditionalize**	Many ancient rituals **were** later **traditionalized in many cultures.**

10	Tranquilize	Zookeepers **tranquilize** animals to prevent them from attacking.
11	Trivialize	The newspaper **trivialized** the events by focusing on their sensational aspects
12	Tyrannize	A cruel dictator **tyrannized** his people.
U		
13	Utilize	The society **is utilizing** a lot of digital gadgets these days
V		
14	Visualize	When it snows, I like **to visualize** vocation on a sunny beach.
15	Vocalize	Mary vocalized her thoughts in singing them out
W		
16	Womanize	Getting dressed like a woman, some men **womanize** themselves.
17	Well-advise	She was **well-advised** to see the doctor.
18	Winterize	I **winterized** my house by putting in storm window

Please, note that when numbering the words we reached the number 100, we started counting them a new. This is a good way to later keep track of the number of the new vocabulary units that you have made yours. The verbs, presented above help economize your speech, and they are very handy in social and business communication.

Enrich your English with some more Adjectives!

3. Helpful Adjectives, Ending in ... "able"

There is more step in word formation that you might find very helpful. It is easy to make as many new adjectives as you need by just adding the ending "a**ble**" **to a verb.** Such adjectives are very handy in speaking, especially when you need to assess a situation or to respond to your partner's comment on something. Be sure to add them to your vocabulary.

Verb + able= Adjective

Verbs:	Adjectives:	Word-Combination:	Examples:
1. To eat	**eatable**	to be eatable	This cheese is not eatable; it's too dry.
2. To drink	**drinkable**	to be drinkable	Thie swamp water is not drinkable.
3. To like	**likable**	to be likable	He is a likable guy.
4. To love	**lovable**	to be lovable	The child is absolutely lovable
5. To believe	**believable**	to be (un believable	It's unbelievable!
6. To explain	**explainable**	to be explainable	It's quite explainable.
7. To accept	**acceptable**	to be (un)acceptable	His behavior is unacceptable
8. to read	**readable**	to be readable	This text is not readable.
9. to drive	**drivable**	to be drivable	This car is not drivable.

10. to teach	**teachable**	to be teachable	\ You live as long as you are teachable.
11. To afford	**affordable**	to be (un) affordable	This house is unaffordable for us,
12. to avail	**available**	to be available	He will not be not available today.
13. to excuse	**excusable**	to be excusable	His behavior is not excusable
14. to fashion	**fashionable**	to be fashionable	It is a very fashionable item.
15. To forget	**unforgettable**	to be unforgettable	My trip was unforgettable
16. To know	**knowledgeable**	to be knowledgeable	He is very knowledgeable.
17. To understand	**understandable**	to be understandable	It's quite understandable.

English is Ruling the World!

You are Ruling Your English!

Post Word

Language has the Legislative Power
In the Brain;
Speech has the Executive Power
In the Mind!

Come to Terms with Both in You!

"If you tap the power of the human brain, there
is no telling what you might do."

Dharmendra Modha - The generator of neural computer

Discover, May 2013

"Right is Might!"

Richard W. Wetherill

Let

The Branches of

Your

"Tree of Knowledge"

Grow

Thanks to English!

Welcome to our website "www.Language Fitness.com

Check out Dr. Ray's books at ***www. drrimalettaray.com***

Knowledge ✚ **Skills**

Intelligence + Consciousness =
Living Intelligence!

29025097R00192

Made in the USA
Middletown, DE
03 February 2016